Melancholy Bay

An Odyssey

Melancholy Bay
An Odyssey

by John Rucker

The East Woods Press
Charlotte, North Carolina
Boston • New York

© 1985 by John Rucker.

Quote on page 89 from "Little Gidding" in FOUR QUARTETS by T.S. Eliot, copyright 1943 by T.S. Eliot; renewed 1971 by Esme Valerie Eliot. Reprinted by permission of Harcourt Brace Jovanovich, Inc. and Faber & Faber Ltd., London.

Text and photography by John Rucker, except for pictures of the author taken by Robert Thornley.

Design, illustration and production by Joy Coleman.

Printed in the United States of America.

All photographs taken with Hasselblad 500C on Ektachrome Professional 120 film.

Special thanks to A Printer's Film Service, Greensboro, N.C.

First printing, 1985

ISBN 0-88742-059-1

Library of Congress Catalog Card Number: 85-045016

Published by The East Woods Press
            Fast & McMillan Publishers, Inc.
            429 East Boulevard
            Charlotte, NC 28203

For my father, a poetic man in a prosaic world.

FOREWORD

Old Barney dozes on the car seat, tenderly covered against a Montana chill, no ordinary spaniel, for John Rucker's diary was written around him. It is the same Barney who retrieved the big rainbows from Alaska rivers, who brought in the Saskatchewan mallards, who monitored the salmon nets and who observed just as intently when a stranger fished by the Jefferson Monument in Washington's cherry blossom time.

There is a feeling that Barney helped plan Rucker's sensitive book and that he is satisfied with his part in it. A dog does not think that way, I am sure, but Rucker's story of America makes nothing trivial, certainly not Barney's part in it. The photographs tell more than they show and Rucker's words probe deep in poetic observation of outdoor space and the people who move in it.

Unusual people write unusual diaries and this is a commercial salmon fisherman who leaves his long nets to cast with a fly rod, sometimes for one small trout. Like many other fly fishermen, this is an observer of nature, literary first; however, technical. As in the pattern of so many fly fishermen he is also a gunner of upland game and waterfowl, but he and Barney move from ruffed grouse to sage hen like other hunters who must see the sweeps of sage and the quaking aspen too without too long a concentration on one scene. Then, of course, there are the chukars of dry mountains along the Snake River.

Rucker, of course, is becoming trapped as travelers of his scarce mold tend to be trapped. Rucker is already entangled in the outdoorsman's snare of needing to visit this river and that mountain each year at a certain time, repetition tending toward what he started out to avoid — a schedule. It is revisiting that gives richness to any scene and this relates to a love for good familiar things like Rucker's one fine shotgun and fine camera with few accessories. He is no collector.

Salmon fishing during the brief Alaska season could be written as a single high adventure but Rucker must go back each year as that frontier becomes a part of his schedule. He and Barney are there for the finest time, however steady the rain or damp their tent, and he assesses with sadness the Eskimo's winters, times of oppressive boredom and even lonely terror. Stark white crosses on a bare northland setting appear more than once in his pictures.

There can be no other diary like Rucker's, of course, for the feelings and experiences are his alone, except for Barney, who probably views them a little differently.

There is no other book like this one — a little bit of regret for fading wilderness, a little melanchololy for far places and a great deal of joy in the outdoors.

Charles F. Waterman

Charles F. Waterman is the author of Fishing in America, The Fisherman's World *and other books on outdoor sport.*

THE ROAD LESS TRAVELLED

You will be accompanying Barney and me from one end of America to the other, from Alaska's Bering Sea to the Atlantic Ocean at the foot of the Cape Hatteras Lighthouse in North Carolina. This journal moves through the four seasons of the year, with the summer taking place in a small Eskimo village that I have called "Melancholy Bay." As a high school teacher, I taught the youths of this village English, and I now spend the summer here as a commercial fisherman. Here the journal asks, "Could all of America's bays and rivers have been this clean and free, only 200 years ago?" As the summer ends, Barney and I follow the ducks, geese and shorebirds as they migrate southward, lingering for six weeks in Montana, Idaho and the Yellowstone Park area. When, in mid-November, the sun has slipped far to the south, and only skirts the low horizon in its daily circuit, we once again join in the migration of thrush and sparrow, catching up with the ever moving fall zone in Arizona. For the winter and spring the narrative moves to the east coast, where Man has had 200 years to try out his boldest experiment, Jeffersonian Democracy. Here the journal asks the question, "Does the free enterprise system lend itself more readily to Man's enlightment or to his greed, and at what cost to the environment we leave to future generations?"

In this journal, which moves from the pristine to the profane, I have tried to share my experiences with the reader in an attempt to give a picture of our country in all its diversity, concentrating on the positive, but also noting the abuses. Its primary purpose is to show parts of our bountiful country that many may not have seen, and from an unusual perspective. During the years that were required to get these pictures and have these true experiences, which are arranged in a chronology of one year, I made an effort to visit each unique environmental habitat-type, ranging from tundra, to short-grass prairie, from desert to barrier island.

Many have had the fantasy, to have the time, to be unencumbered, to ramble across the continent, making a diversion whenever a river or a canyon beckoned. And all with the companionship of a friend who is intelligent, curious and blissfully silent.

My belief is that each of us is a fisherman, some simply have not been led to the waters. Many think fishing means staring at a cork or blasting across a reservoir in a speedboat, watching an electronic fish finder. Once one has been led to the quiet waters, the rod and line become the umbilical cord to that which we all yearn for, serenity. Given Man's curious nature and his love of a puzzle, the act of fishing becomes almost self-evident. During the dawn of history, the shadow of Man and his fishing rod was cast upon the waters.

Join Barney and me, then, on a fishing quest, a trip to the headwaters of Man's innocence, and his guilt.

J.R.
April, 1984
Victoria, British Columbia

Melancholy Bay

An Odyssey

Walrus — Bristol Bay, Alaska

Summer
Alaska

June 1— I have learned that Simeon is dead.

I have learned that Simeon is dead.

Whiskey did what no winter white-out, no summer gale could do; took you away from the hills, the bay, the river you loved. Friends have told me that you had been drinking while you were in Dillingham, and that your snowmachine went through the ice near the Togiak River, as you returned to Melancholy Bay. You were the first villager to befriend me. When I was new to the bay and let the wind blow me up on a mud flat as the tide went out, you came to help and your propeller fouled in my net. We stood with the waves washing over the tops of our hip boots, unwrapping my net from your prop. You said over and over to me, "I'm so very sorry."

Once I carried you, as light and small boned as a child, in my arms into your tarpapered shack after you had been drinking. As I lay you on the tiny bed where you slept alone, you muttered "son-a-bitch, son-a-bitch," in your broken English. I never knew if you were talking about yourself or me. Now your sister will have no more beaver to make her hats and mittens to sell, no more ptarmigan that you caught by stringing salmon netting across the narrow passes where the grouse-like birds trade back and forth in winter. Your mother still walks the village in her faded kuspak, thin scarf over her white hair, but the light is gone from her face. Her bonnie boy and my friend of few words, is gone forever.

June 3 — I have accounted for all the intrepid fliers...

I have accounted for all the intrepid fliers that do not wait for summer but come in on the leading edge of the spring thaw. The swans are back and are nearly indistinguishable from the snow banks that mottle these hinterlands and fill the landscape with a tinkling sonority as they melt and trickle away. These great birds express their joy of arriving here on the nesting grounds by maple-leafing, falling from the sky in wild, twisting flight. The drake pintails, the lesser Canadian geese and the golden plover find the ponds and lakes which have thawed, even though the majority are still in the grip of winter. The little common snipe can be heard high overhead, one of the first sounds of life returning to the tundra. His wingbeats, as he pulls out of his endless dives, make a faraway winnowing sound. I make a silent promise to the birds, whose every action mirrors their determination to succeed in the difficult task that lies before them, that I will not leave this sad and lovely place before they do.

June 4 — I sit on a tarp,

I sit on a tarp, each of my three outboard motors partly disassembled before me. One needs lower unit seals, another a new forward gear, and the third has a warped cylinder head. The parts I have brought seem toylike and endearing, viewed against the random, overpowering landscape. On this day the bay is nearly turquoise, the color of the back of a sockeye salmon or "blueback" before he comes into fresh water. The high tide wind, smelling faintly of seaweed and rotting fish, has battalions of whitecaps marching in formation across this little notch in Alaska's southwest coast.

When I left last September, my energy reserves gone from nearly five months of herring and salmon fishing, all three motors had failed and I hadn't the strength to fix them. Now the sins of last fall weigh heavy on my shoulders. Will the parts and special tools I brought be the right ones? The commercial salmon periods begin in a week.

The birds are busy too. I watch two black-cheeked male lapland longspurs wage war hour after hour, ignoring wind and cold. Every whistled melody is a challenge to combat. Each bird knows that winning a female, when they arrive in two weeks, will depend on having a quarter acre of tundra free from the claims of all other male lapland longspurs. Several times, one or the other sparrow-sized birds lands on the resting Barney. His brown and white coat is exactly the same color as the pre-summer tundra. He does not open his eyes, knowing full well who the pests are. By September Barney will be bleached auburn from the twenty hour a day sun, and I will have shed ten pounds gained during last winter's boredom and lost sense of purpose.

June 7—Took my first trip upriver for the season,

Took my first trip upriver for the season, running up about ten miles. Walked to the top of Lookout Mountain. From where I sit, the river is a ribbon of silver which wanders through the empty, silent valley like a truant school boy. The willow and alder buds are just beginning to form. Barney runs up to me where I sit, his paws and face black from arctic ground squirrel digs, red tongue and gums flecked with dirt, eyes on fire. Returning to the boat, he bounces along ahead of me in a peculiar rocking horse fashion on the spongy tundra.

June 12 — After two days of hauling gear up the hill...

After two days of hauling gear up the hill and then over a bumpy trail in a wheelbarrow, I have finished setting up my camp for the summer. My tent stands in the same place as last year; in a depression on the hillside that gives some protection from the storms that blow out of the southeast. A spring issues from among the roots of alders and willows of the thicket that nearly surrounds my tent. I have scooped out a hole to make the dipping of drinking water easier. The achingly cold water spurts from the bottom of the pool from three ever swirling nipples of sand.

June 13 — One of the great pleasures of the summer...

One of the great pleasures of the summer in Melancholy Bay is walking the two miles from camp into the village on the gravel path that winds down the hill to the airstrip. Many of the Eskimo kids of the village speak of me as "the gussack who comes up with Barney each summer." Today a group of boys stand outside the village store as I walk by. One asks my why Barney has no tail. "Because that's the way the '73 models came," I tell him. In a world where the barge and the cargo plane bring snowmobiles, outboard motors, and the various new machines of the year, this makes perfectly good sense. The solemn faces nod and study the fascinating stub of Barney's tail. Only one looks at me quizzically, a slight hint of mirth about his eyes. Barney himself is delighted to be back to this place that he regards as a vast smorgasbord of bones, skins, and salmon heads, complete with tender shoots of green grass to sooth his culture-shocked stomach.

I walk past plywood houses where dyed seal intestine, to be used by the women in weaving designs in their grass baskets, hangs from the clothesline. King salmon strips dry in the sun and wind, hopefully before the flies come. All, including man, struggle to meet one deadline after another before the ice fastens its chains around Melancholy Bay for the winter.

Returning to camp, there is a shrill whistle from a nearby hillock. Ever a thorn in Barney's side, the arctic ground squirrel, or to use the common name given by the Eskimos, the "parka squirrel," that lives there misses no opportunity to torment him as we pass. The tundra drums with Barney's gallop as he runs to the hole where the squirrel has disappeared. After a few minutes' half-hearted digging, he catches up with me on the path. His familiar brown and white back, broad and wooly, so like an enormous caterpillar, once more resumes its normal place before my eyes. In

September, when we fish during the day instead of all night, I will walk this same trail in the dark after the day's work is done, and will depend on Barney's dim, moving form to guide my steps. Often I cannot keep up with him and he is swallowed up by the night. I stand and wait for him to return to me and lead me the rest of the way to the tent. He startles me when suddenly his brown and white form appears at my feet in the darkness.

June 14 — Feels good to be back;

Feels good to be back; all my equipment is working; my belt already taken in several holes; hair cut short; hands hard. Last night, during the first commercial opening, watched the towering gray mass of a thunderstorm move up the valley of the Melancholy River, toward the bay. Took in the boat with a rushing of wind, cold and stony, the very breath of the Kilbuck Mountains, and large, pelting raindrops. In ten minutes the thick black column of water has left me in a blissful calm and I watch it sweep over the boats off Beluga Rock. One hour later I can see it far out at sea, trailing its whispy mare's tail of rain behind. Caught some truly grand king salmon tonight, some better than forty pounds. As I pull them alongside, I stare down into their handsome silver mouths, open in shock; lives ended within sight of their parent river, the Melancholy, after trailing her sweet waters to this point from hundreds of miles out at sea. Many are marked with seal bites. I swing them into the boat with a groan where they flop heavily on the deck. I am out of breath with the waste and extravagance of the moment, with my inability to stem life's rapacity. As they hit the net, they pull thirty feet of cork line underwater and beat the water mightily, the energy waiting to be spent on the Melancholy's current as they seek the exact spot where they themselves were born, and in propagation, instead wasted on this insidious, ensnaring web. I say silently, "Die without struggling, somehow make yourself less pure. You are far grander than we who kill you."

June 16 — The songbirds appear so frail,

The songbirds appear so frail, ill-equipped for survival in such a harsh environment. I wonder how they ever complete the migration to and from Alaska each summer. While the big airships, the geese and swans, cross the bay in stiff winds without a compass point's variance from course, the savanna sparrows, the yellow wagtails, and the water pipits, are buffeted by the capricious gusts. They flit from alder to willow seeming to abhor open spaces where the wind can ravage them. I imagine these tiny bits of down in night flight over a wind-whipped ocean and wonder how such a thing can be.

June 20 — After preparing for tomorrow's commercial opening,

After preparing for tomorrow's commercial opening, I put rainsuit, bird field guide and binoculars into my backpack and rambled away the afternoon. Found markers, either rock cairns or two sticks stuck into the ground to form an inverted "v" indicating berry picking areas or ground squirrel colonies, which the women trap in order to make fur parkas. I pick up a rusty five gallon can to see how clever hands have fashioned it into a camp stove. Looking inside, I see a small nest made of merganser breast feathers and grass in the corner of the can and two tiny, broken eggs, yolks running into the other corner. A pair of yellow wagtails flit like bits of electricity in a nearby thicket. Sadly, I realize that an observer with the best of intentions, has an impact on his surroundings by his mere presence.

June 21 — Had a full load just as the sky began to lighten up.

Had a full load just as the sky began to lighten up. Nosed the boat up on the beach to wait with the other boats already there to be unloaded. Village kids, splattered with mud and fish blood throw the salmon from the boats into plastic tubs and drag them up the beach to scales, where they are weighed and dumped into large aluminum bins. The fishermen stand by their boats, rain gear glistening. The DC-3, dull silver in the 3:00 a.m. light, waits like a huge alien craft, its bay doors flung open to receive the aluminum bins of salmon. Ten year old Danny Wassillie kneels in a plastic fish tub and paddles it around the twenty-four foot plywood boat built by his father, oblivious to the weather and the hour. The Wassillies' six sled dog puppies have found their way to the beach at "the point" and Danny splashes them with the piece of plank-ing he uses as a paddle and tells them, in Yupik, to go home, but the puppies ignore him. The kids unloading the fish trip over the frolicking pups in the poor light and fall, laughing, to the wet sand.

The DC-3 is full now, overloaded in fact, and his engines cough red flames as he rolls to the end of the runway. He sits idling for twenty minutes, facing his adversary, a short, soft runway, warming the engines which must not hestitate when he lifts off. Finally, engines roaring, he runs down the strip which ends abruptly in Melancholy Bay a scant few hundred yards ahead, blasting huge puddles into mist, wings flapping alarmingly. The thunder of his engines dwarfs all undertakings of man and nature at that moment and all eyes are on him as he lifts ponderously off the ground and turns, slow and huge, over the bay. The running lights are glimpsed through holes in the low clouds like pulsating jewels in the sky. I watch until they flicker out. I look around and notice that everyone is gone; Danny and his father, the puppies, the village kids; all swallowed up by the mist. I hear the anchors of boats off the point splash heavily. It is nearly 6:00 a.m.; not enough time for another drift on the incoming tide. I begin the long walk up the hill to the tent.

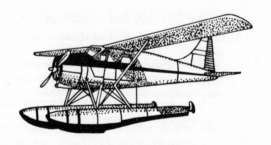

June 22 — Went upriver for the weekend.

Went upriver for the weekend. Since the bears are still on the hill-sides and few are on the river now, I leave the rifle behind; one less piece of equipment to worry about. I have to laugh to myself when I think of how I envisioned that life in the roadless part of Alaska I am in, would be simpler than in Montana. A float trip there had been as easy as leaving a car at a bridge and floating down to it. Up here, power is needed to get people up rivers, either with outboard motor or with float plane. First I take twelve gallons of gas in a wheelbarrow to the point and then change to the stainless steel prop, worn to considerably less than its original size by the gravel on the riverbed. Next I load up the little bug-proof tent, sleeping bag and pad, tool box, critical spare parts, peanut butter, pilot bread, butter, salt, frying pan, cook stove, white gas, camera equip-ment, fishing gear, waders, and felt-soled wading shoes, and cover it all with a tarp. Ironically, here where there are often no people to help when one is in trouble, there is more reliance on technology than in the lower 48 states, where an endless support community makes such preparations unnecessary, even though I came to Alaska primarily to escape technology and its encroachments.

I run upriver about fifteen miles and discover while setting up camp that I have left the most important accoutrement of the camper, insect repellent. There will be no protection for the backs of my hands and my face, nor for Barney's eyebrows and base of nose. That night I lie in the tent in the semi-darkness and listen to the splashing of working beavers, rolling salmon, the slow, even breathing of Barney, the whine of mosquitos outside the tent, the seductive sound of the river. I find myself longing for the sound of a human voice. I promise myself I will buy a portable A.M. radio with long range circuitry, capable of picking up Dillingham, for next summer. Alaska is a bad place for the purist.

At some point I think I hear Barney growl softly but I do not bother with unzipping the entrance to the tent, for I do not want to let any mosquitos in. The next morning I am out early, eager to work the riffle in front of the island where I am camped before the rainbow trout move into the deep pools where they hold during the brightest part of the day. In the tall grass, still dripping wet with dew, a trail has been mashed flat where a grizzly bear has passed through. The paw prints in the sand disappear into the river ten feet from the tent, where he entered to swim across.

June 23 — Fly rod in hand,

Fly rod in hand, small pebbles and sand under the arch of my foot inside my wading shoes makes walking very unpleasant as I quietly shadow my "mystery bird," a thrush of some variety; a Swainson's, a hermit or a grey-faced. When he appears momentarily in view in the dense willow thicket, I watch intently for a tail dipping motion that will identify him as a hermit thrush, but either he is not a hermit or he deliberately beguiles me. Seeing a grey-black wall of rain approaching underneath a horizon of thunderclouds, I pull the sixteen foot skiff out as far as I can on a gravel bar and lie under the leeward side of the boat as the windblown raindrops first plop tentatively, then rattle cheerily on the boat, and then in a joyous rush, spray the gravel, the river, the skiff and the willows with a raking fire of cold, perfect droplets which roll momentarily on the dark surface of the river like thousands of tiny, white pearls. Barney huddles at my feet, hugging the side of the boat as I do. I laugh my "how do we always get in situations like this?" laugh and he looks away in wet disgust. I study the glistening pebbles beneath my nose in the reverberating silence after the rain passes.

My mystery bird has vanished and I wander downriver, looking for anything of interest in the dripping riverine world. I take short cuts across the small islands which the river has created as the water drops with each passing week. Barney seeks out the little ponds that have been cut off from the river and chases the doomed salmon fry that dart about. Small flocks of phalarope and sandpiper flash by. These are celibate birds that were unable to compete and win mates or have had their broods destroyed.

Side by side the successful and the guiltfree unsuccessful live out their days, each in its own way, making a contribution, for if all succeeded, the resulting overpopulation would be disastrous.

"I think I could turn and live with the animals, they are so placid
    and self-contained.
I stand and look at them long and long
They do not sweat and whine about their condition
They do not lie awake in the dark and weep for their sins
They do not make me sick discussing their duty to God.
No one is dissatisfied, no one is demented with the mania of
    owning things
No one kneels to another, nor to his kind that lived thousands of
    years ago.
No one is respectable or industrious over the whole earth."

"Song of Myself," Walt Whitman

June 24 – Fly fishing without using the first finger on either hand is difficult.

Fly fishing without using the first finger on either hand is difficult.
The crease where each joint bends has become open and raw from
pulling in the gill nets and handling kings, reds, and chums, but
the fish are feeding on this overcast, blustery day. One thunderstorm after another rolls down the valley of the Melancholy River,
but in between them my fly reel protests as line is stripped off by
large rainbow trout. I am ahead of the chums and Dolly Varden
trout that will soon be in this part of the river, and I know each
strike to be a rainbow or occasionally, a grayling. I watch the
homing king salmon pushing a hump of water through the riffle
that runs past my tent on their way further upriver to spawn. I keep
the flies away from them for I do not want the thirty and forty
pound fish to strip the line down to the backing, and break it,
taking my only seven weight fly line. I fish a pair of flies, a bright
orange Babine special or "egg fly" on the dropper as an attractor,
and a large Muddler minnow, tied seductively with yarn and rabbit
fur, as the tail fly. I am intently curious to see which fly has scored
each time the pair has its gentle downstream swing interrupted
with a jarring strike. I wade across a deep hole that takes me up to
the belt on my chest waders. Barney swims at my side; so clear is
the water that he seems to be supported in air. We both climb out
at a beaver house as tall as I am. Standing on the side of it, I can
see a pair of rainbows holding in front of a boulder-sized chunk of
tundra which has fallen into the river and rests on the bottom.
They are both handsome fish; the larger one should go five
pounds. I swing the flies past and their mouths flash white as they
nip at the shiny split shot sinkers that are pinched onto the leader,

but they are not interested in my offerings. I tie on a streamer with a bright silver tinsel body, hoping this will appeal to them, but again they only nip at the split shots. I go through my entire large fly box, but the only motion is the steady wag of the rear one-third of Barney's dripping wet body as he stands at my side, watching it all.

In desperation I tie on a Colorado spinner, hoping the little flashing blade will appeal to this fish's fancy, but he only stares stonily ahead. As I snap the lid shut on my last fly box, the larger fish seems to levitate to the surface, taking a floating morsel with a delicate sip. From a seldom used pouch in my vest, I extract a small box of deer hair bass bugs, each the size of a mouse. I seldom use them since they are difficult to cast, but occasionally the big rainbows, thinking them to be a vole, or perhaps a lemming that has fallen into the river, will take them.

In a very real sense, the "mouse;" which is the gussack name given by the native people to all types of voles, lemmings and shrews; could be considered the patron saint of the Melancholy rainbows. It has long been held as dogma among the old people of this area that since rainbow trout will eat "mice," they are unfit for human consumption. This is fortunate indeed, for when the Melancholy's population of trout concentrates for the winter in the big pools at the mouth of the river, they could be wiped out by jigging or subsistence gill nets hung under the ice. Instead, the Dolly Varden trout is the targeted species for winter food, and there is an almost endless supply of them since, like the salmon, they do much of their feeding and growing in the sea.

The fly settles softly several yards above the larger fish and is taken with supreme confidence as it passes over him. I lead him downstream about fifty yards, lifting the rod over willows, moving as quickly as possible through the tall grass and along the broken, uneven riverbank, to a long, safe riffle, where he sulks in the heavy current in several feet of water. Not wanting to overly tire him, I soon lay the fish on his side for Barney to retrieve. He is surprised by the fish's girth, and misses on the first pass, but takes him on the second. I gently remove the prize from Barney's jaws before he can get out of the water with it and am instantly showered as he shakes to show his irritation at being robbed of a fish that, in Barney's mind, he had caught without any help from me. This is standard procedure with Barney and me; all I can do is to try to turn my face in time to save my glasses from the spray. Holding the fish in the current, I note that he is fully four fingers thick across the back; the best fish of the day. Since nonanadromous trout this far north are limited to a very short growing season, these Melancholy rainbows are much too precious to kill. This particular fish may have taken eight years to reach his weight. I release him and he rights himself immediately, drifts downstream several feet with the current, then darts away.

Barney and I return to the beaver lodge to try for the second fish, but he has been disturbed and has moved away, but there is a grayling in the same place, his iridescent dorsal fin trailing along his back like a black cape. I have switched back to my favorite combination of flies and he takes the tail fly on the first pass. Weighing only a pound, I am able to hold him safely in spite of the roots and branches in the water and Barney makes a clean grab. I admire the fin of the fish that the French call L'Ombre, "The Shadow." He will be kept for supper. The white fillets will be a welcome change from the rich red salmon Barney and I have eaten all week.

It is now 9:00 p.m. and I have one more hour of fishing time remaining. I slosh downstream to a meandering braid that leaves the main course of the river. I like these charming little rivulets that wander through the flood plain and return to the main channel. They are the same size as the little creeks of Montana where I fish the worm on short leader for brook trout, but here they hold rainbows that startle me with their brightness, bigness and suddenness.

I fish fifty yards, the braid only eight or ten feet across; the willows making a backcast very difficult; moving several fish that make my heart race. Grizzly bears like these braids too for here they know they are less likely to encounter Man. As I cut across a meander, pushing my way through grass that comes up to my eyes, I find I am suddenly standing in a bear bed, the grass mashed flat. I touch it and it is hot and the musky smell of bear hangs heavy in the air. I walk slowly through my own trail in the grass, out to the tinkling innocence of the braid, the hair standing up on the back of my neck. Barney urinates in the bed and then quickly follows me. I begin to splash my way back to the camp, whistling loudly. I decide that I must discard my theory about the bears still being on the hillsides.

July 1 — Today July blew in out of the southeast...

Today July blew in out of the southeast at forty knots, the tattered orange nylon windsock standing straight out like the flame of a blow torch. The mail plane came in against the crosswind like a crab swimming through air, the wings of the twin engine Otter going parallel to the ground only moments before the wheels touched the runway. It was very difficult to walk into town against the wind. In front of the Post Office there are nearly a hundred large propane tanks, as tall as I am. Each one has a hole in its cap and when the wind blows hard, a strange moaning is heard throughout the village. I call them "the Martians," each with its single eye and unearthly voice. I hear them talking behind my back as I head up the hill, where I hope my canvas wall tent is still staked to the ground.

July 2 — Nature seems eager to have back the metals...

Nature seems eager to have back the metals taken from her ores. She ignores the machines that are man's pride and joy as they run smoothly for a short while, then salt, sand, and time freeze the turning wheels. "We'll have you back now," the wind whispers. A Caterpillar tractor, growling its potency only a few years ago, now has sparrows nesting in its diesel engine compartment, and grass pokes up through the rust fused treads.

From the air I see abandoned snow machines on the tundra, scores of miles from the nearest village. I wonder, each time; was the Eskimo whose machine failed travelling alone? Did he make it back to his village on foot? Do his mouse-gnawed bones lie somewhere in the vastness below? Did the wind whisper in his ear, "We'll have you back now."?

July 3 — Fished the tail end of the big blow;

Fished the tail end of the big blow; the bay very roily; much grass in the net. It seems each time a rain cloud passes overhead and large drops begin to pelt my rain gear, a dozen fish strike the net and the white corks dance. Watched "Hopeless" drifting his net near my boat. Hopeless is a fellow from Hope, a town near Anchorage, who started fishing Melancholy Bay this summer. He always fishes in the wrong place on the wrong tide, takes twice as long to pull in his net as anyone else, but nevertheless I envy him more than any other fisherman on the bay. His puller is his wife, who seems to grow more maddeningly beautiful with the passing of each lonely week. Living in unspoiled country is easy enough; finding a woman who can stand it is the real challenge.

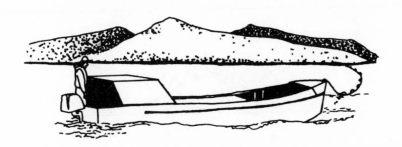

July 6 — On my canvas roof, there is rain that rattles...

On my canvas roof, there is rain that rattles and rain that drums.
There is wind that pops the walls like a sail, and wind that rustles
the nearby willows like a passing ghost. On windless nights there
are mosquitoes that hum like the distant dynamos of Hell. On
these deadly nights, I pitch the little bug proof tent inside the
canvas wall tent, a tent within a tent. When I zip up the fly, I hunt
down the hapless ones that have slipped in with Barney and me,
one at a time. Dozens of dried splotches, where I have mashed
individuals engorged with my blood or Barney's, against the nylon
walls, are testimony of my thoroughness.

July 7 — No fishing today. Put the chair outside...

No fishing today. Put the chair outside the tent and read through the morning. Watched as two Eskimo lovers from the village walk to the top of a distant hillside, and stand looking over their harsh, wind cleansed Garden of Eden, two tiny figures that became one as they embraced. Less than halfway through the summer and I'm already painfully lonely. Most of the birds have paired off. A golden crowned sparrow lands on the tent pole and says, with his usual three sad, falling notes, "O Dear Me."

Spent the afternoon repairing with fiberglass. Today the drone of the flies is the voice of the bay; wind is sleeping. From the rotting carcasses of walrus, seal, and salmon, the energetic maggots have metamorphosed and taken to wing. On the sun struck surfaces of each boat, their backs are emerald. The tide has left my boat high and dry where boats have been beached for two thousand years, at "the point," historic site of the village of Melancholy Bay. As I work, Barney, as he often does, plays with a stick, growling and tossing it into the air. I notice that it is strangely shaped. I find it is a piece of preserved reindeer horn, turned into a wood splitting tool with end splintered with pounding by hands that worked, ages ago, where I work on this day. In the handle of the eight inch piece is a hole, perhaps a drill seat. I kick in the sand near the boat and find another artifact, a piece of bone armor from a breast shield of interlocking bone plates, and also a rough chipped stone chopping tool, so perfectly shaped to the hand that my fingers naturally find their intended position. The salmon skin rain gear, that unlike plastic, did not sweat inside, the loon skin ceremonial parkas, the hand-woven traps for the blackfish that live in the tundra ponds, all reflect the musicality of the relationship these people had with their environment. Was it lack of imagination that held them within the orbit of the natural cycle, or was it an atavistic wisdom? I try to imagine an archeologist of some description two thousand years hence, handling an artifact of today, a telephone receiver or a television cabinet and perhaps saying, "Ah, it was at this point that they began to close the door, not only to each other, but also to their only home, the verdant earth."

July 9 — Today's fishing period ended just as a black storm...

Today's fishing period ended just as a black storm front moved to the head of the bay. Each boat pulled in its net at 6:00 a.m., seemed to study its foe for a minute while rocking in the building swell, and then slowly headed toward the storm building at the other end of the bay, where a processing barge, the only buyer working the bay this week, lay at anchor. My boat has a load of just under a ton of salmon. My helper is bailing before we have covered two hundred yards, with twelve and a half miles to go. Crossing the bay against thirty-five knots of wind, I don't see many smiles on the faces that pass by in faster boats. My glasses beaded with water, I watch the crests of nearby waves being blown off, deadly, invisible fingers seeming to play on the dark water. Standing with my face into the wind, I monitor the throb of the engines through my hand as I steer the boat. Barney is curled up inside the little plywood cabin. Every time spray rattles on the windows he curls up into a yet tighter ball.

July 10 — As I put on my pack outside the tent,

As I put on my pack outside the tent, watched what to me is the most extraordinary courtship flight of all the birds that breed here, that of the semi-palmated plover. As he emits a single, endlessly repeated "peep," he attempts to attract a female by his strange flight, apparently feeling that the more batlike and erratic it is, the more appealing he is. His flight can only be described as hyper-indecisive, for one wingbeat carries him forward, the next to the left, the next to the right, then up, then down; every direction save backward. While it is dizzying and bewildering to me to watch, to the shy female it must be sheer aphrodisiac.

At the bottom of the hill in the pond along the airstrip are half a dozen northern phalaropes. I watch their fascinating habit of swimming rapidly in small circles, tittering excitedly all the while. Inexplicably, the birds have reversed sex-roles, the females have the bright colors, and defend the nest, while the drab male raises the young. Though they have a light-boned delicacy that suggests a swallow, they are pelagic for much of the year, spending the winter on the high seas.

Near the village, I am confronted by a tiny, western sandpiper. She frets nervously on the tundra just off the path where I stand, flashing the silver underside of her wing as a warning that I am near her brood. She has no time for me, and as soon as I am safely past, she disappears in the tussocks of grass where her little ones hide, seeming to be very upset at loosing those few precious seconds in the tutelage of her chicks.

Each summer when I return, I see I have been tricked, during the winter spent in "civilization," into believing that time has turned benign, has become more forgiving. In a setting where Man has replaced all things natural with things manmade, and Man himself sits at the center of this microcosm, the natural world outside the gates is soon regarded as extraneous. Our sense of natural rhythms and even the duration and importance of our own lives becomes distorted. Each summer as I watch the salmon, the brief flowers, even the mosquitos, complete their cycles and die, I am reminded that my cycle is brief, too. In Melancholy Bay all things are viewed in terms of cycles of seasons. An outboard motor or a skiff has one, maybe two, summers left in it. Dan tells me his oldest and smartest sled dog has one more winter left. I find myself wondering if Simeon's mother will live until next spring.

The villagers seem to regard the present not as a distinct entity, but rather as a point on a circle. George Sanders once told me that when he first came to Melancholy Bay with the military to make weather observations after World War II, one of the old villagers had, seeing a wristwatch for the first time, pointed to the dial of George's watch and said, "Sun comes up here, high here, and goes down here," easily making the connection with the dial and the passing moments of the day. Had that old man, born and raised in a true stone age culture, seen today's digital watch flashing the isolated minutes, removed entirely from the context of the cycle of the day, I do not think it would have had any more significance to him than it would have to Barney.

Time here is redefined and compressed to its true dimensions. Its nature is personified by the creatures that labor under the draconian schedules. From the perspective of North Carolina, my life seems to stretch almost endlessly into the future, from Montana somewhat less, but from the perspective of Melancholy Bay, it seems that the few yearly cycles that remain to me could be held in the palm of my hand. I watch the children at play, the puppies born this summer, the birds of the year. I watch the old women who seek berries on the hillsides, the white-muzzled sled dogs that will not survive the coming winter. It is seen and accepted by everyone from the village elders to the village idiot that we are each swept along by the same tide and it is useless to try to swim against it.

July 15 — Fished all night; misty and calm.

Fished all night; misty and calm. Nick Andrew and his partner came alongside to ask for white gas for their cookstove, smelling of whiskey. Nick smiled dreamily and said, "Ceiling less than one mile; no Fish and Game float plane will patrol tonight." For the next hour we drift side by side, the red buoys at the ends of our nets almost touching. He drifts his net in haphazard fashion, making no effort to keep it straight. As I pull in my net at the boundary marker, he continues to drift in slowly with the incoming tide. Hours later I hear wild laughter coming out of the mist a mile inside the boundary, almost in the river itself, and the splash of heavy kings in Nick's net.

Last winter he took his snowmachine from Melancholy Bay through the Kilbuck Mountains, up the frozen Kuskokwim River to hunt moose. He does not own a compass. Hunting ptarmigan in March, he is frequently gone for a week at a time, alone on his snowmachine, pulling his sled behind, threading the unnamed passes of the Kilbuck Range. Nick thinks nothing of his sense of direction, only becomes embarassed when I ask him how he does it. If I tried to tell Nick that he is the last of the line of instinctive navigators who led his fellow man over the Siberian land bridge 11,000 years ago, and across Alaska, he would probably laugh politely and make up an excuse to leave. His gift is overshadowed by the great jets that leave contrails in the sky, bound for Japan from Anchorage. His fellow hunters in the village know him for what he is, but the homage which should be his is given to the pilots of the thundering DC-3's. Nick, the bearer of a nearly extinct and mystical gift, gift, lives alone in one of the poorest shacks in the village among the people whose creed has been "Be clever to survive" in this harsh land that does not suffer fools and slow learners, since before the time my own ancestors huddled in fear through the Dark Ages.

While pouring the white gas through a funnel into his cookstove, I ask him if he knows there is a plan to build a barge port at the mouth of Melancholy Bay. "It'll change your way of life forever," I tell him. He smiles, showing his teeth, rotten from eating candy, "Will they build a bar?"

July 17—At 5:00 a.m. I am awakened by the white crowned...

At 5:00 a.m. I am awakened by the white crowned and golden crowned sparrows as they drink at the spring and then perch on the tent's ridge pole and on the ropes. Like muffled alarm clocks the brief bursts of whirring wingbeats sound one after another until all the birds that sleep in the thicket that surrounds my tent, have left to forage. Although it is only the middle of July, the male lapland longspurs have lost their sporty courting colors. They are nearly indistinguishable from the drab females which blend perfectly with the mottled landscape. Great flocks of them spring up like locusts as I walk into the village. From the direction of Little Beluga Rock the peculiar call of nesting arctic loons rises and falls sporadically, a background noise that seems to issue from the sky.

In June there was only a string of stars directly overhead, like a map of a subway line, the sky elsewhere being too light all hours of the four hour "night." But last evening the skies blew clear of clouds for several hours and I saw that the string of stars had widened to a band. I lie on my back on the spongy, living mat of tundra and gaze at them, taking great pleasure from the moment. I am watching for Vega, who dances over my tent half of each summer, to appear any week now, as more and more stars emerge in the darkening skies. I am only one of many stargazers on this night. The young sparrows, thrushes, and warblers of my hillside, who will make the long jumps of their migration at night, are imprinting the constellations for use as navigational aids. I imagine the consciousness of a trillion organisms creating an ethereal veil of radiating energy that envelopes Earth like the filaments spun by the spiders in a field of grass. And so I lie and send up my light's pinpoint of energy, like a note in a bottle upon an uncharted sea.

July 23 — Went upriver for the night. I run the skiff...

Went upriver for the night. I run the skiff at twenty miles per hour, as Barney stands like a figurehead at the bow. In the utterly clear water, he cranes to watch the swarms of Dolly Varden trout and sockeye salmon that hang along the cut banks. Camped in one of my favorite places, an abandoned village site that I think of as "the place of the beautiful children." The tall grass, which has claimed the mounds and sunken dwelling of the ancient village, is full of ghosts. The families that used to live here along the river have all moved away to the village of Melancholy Bay, for schools, groceries, and recently, T.V. This lonely place, visited only by the occasional fox and bear and Barney and me, once rippled with laughter. Pretty, round-faced children grew up eating salmon and berries, fearing only starvation and bears. Nearby, not far from the tall grass, a single white cross remains standing, surrounded by rusted pots and kettles to be used by the deceased in his journey through eternity.

Last week I walked into the plywood house of an Eskimo friend in the village of Melancholy Bay and found the beautiful children there, with bottles of soft drink and candy in their hands, watching "The Exorcist" in wonderment on home video. Babes, you are flung into the bottomless well of consumerism without survival skills. In this new wilderness, all the lodestars to which you turned your eyes in the past, are eclipsed. Lovely creatures, the world cannot wait for you.

"We Nations of Europe, I thought, who do not fear to flood-light our own inmost mechanisms, are here turning the blazing lights of our civilization into dark eyes, fitly set like the eyes of doves by the rivers of waters (Song of Solomon 5:12), essentially different to ours. If for a long enough time we continue in this way to dazzle and blind the Africans, we may in the end bring upon them a longing for darkness, which will drive them into the gorges of their own, unknown mountains and their own, unknown minds."

Shadows on the Grass, Isak Dinesen

July 29 — From my hillside, half a mile above the airstrip,

From my hillside, half a mile above the airstrip, I watch the comings and goings of each aircraft that drops from the clouds that seem to be foundered upon the spires and headlands standing like sentries around Melancholy Bay. The DC-3's are sometimes so full of iced salmon that they lumber down the short, gravel runway and appear to become airborne only when they roll off the end, where the ten foot drop of the built-up gravel strip gives them air under their wings. They turn, huge and absurd, like some great flightless bird gone mad in an attempt to regain the firmament.

Last week, during a storm out of the southeast, I poked my head between the wet canvas flaps of the tent and squinted into the stinging rain, watching the Department of Fish and Game's red and white float plane, with pontoons for landing on water, as it doggedly searched for a level where the forty knot wind would grant easier passage. The pontoons cause much friction against the wind that snakes over my hillside like a stampeding herd of aeolian buffalo. His is a lonely job at the moment. The heavens are in discord and the bay and air above the bay move as in a great tuning of instruments, seeking a lost harmony. I watch the float plane, tiny in the distance now, buffeted like a bit of thistledown, but still making way. The ground under my feet feels very sweet.

As varied as Chaucer's pilgrims, they drop the nose and cut power. "Tail draggers" with balloon tires that land on remote, soft-sand beaches to pick up salmon from commercial set netters, Twin Otters that seem to hop vertically into the air after using only fifty yards of runway, "flying boxcars," even an occasional antique Grumman Goose. Most are strictly utilitarian, built for barging freight through the skies. I marvel at the skill of the air taxi and air charter pilots. They have left backgrounds as varied as a summer's experiences on Melancholy Bay, to fly these wild skies. They are disillusioned intellectuals, Vietnam veterans, dreamers fleeing boredom, all hopelessly lost in their love affair with the wind. They woo her like responsive, skillful lovers, testing her mood with a light feathering of the controls.

Standing by the airstrip on the way to my tent I cover my ears to muffle the rattling, metallic drone of their propellers as they run down the gravel strip, trailing a plume of dust as they build up speed to lift a heavy load of bundled passengers. They tilt the wings and lift one tire from the runway as if testing the new element, one wheel in the heavens even as the other one is still touching the earth, then leap into the air with a lurching motion that can only be described as do or die. Last week a wealthy Anchorage sport fisherman dropped in out of a clear and breezy sky in an expensive prop plane with retractable landing gear. I watched him fly the course of the river, looking for pods of salmon, banking and turning with the caprice and whimsey of a swallow, making my heart ache.

August 1 — Lay in my sleeping bag last night, listening...

Lay in my sleeping bag last night listening to the right wall of the tent flapping in the wind; woke to find it had shifted during the night, and was now blowing in, very cold, under the front flaps. Standing outside and stretching, saw two of the old women from the village out picking berries already on the next hillside. Walked into the village to check for mail, passing Oscar James pushing a full fifty-five gallon drum of stove oil to his house by butting it with the front tire of his three wheeler. Dan's sled dogs create a terrible din as Barney trots by. He knows they would like to tear him to bits, so jealous are they of his freedom. He does not look at them.

I think of last summer when Barney let me perform a bit of crude dentistry on him. He had fought with his archenemy, Jughead, and in the wild snapping of jaws, he had knocked out a tooth against the younger teeth of Jughead. The tooth had dangled by a piece of gum, and not wanting Barney to inhale it into his lungs, I had held his mouth open and snipped it out with the scissors on my Swiss Army knife. I look at Dan's sled dogs, Malamutes, Siberian huskies, but mostly wiry, indefatigable mongrels, straining at their chains, mired in mud, faces ravaged by mosquitos and gnats, and shudder at the thought of such an operation on one of them.

Back at the tent, I tenderly open my mail and read the endearing messages written on folded pieces of white paper; they are more important to me than all the beauty and grandeur that stand outside my canvas walls.

August 4 – It is a lonely walk into the village.

It is a lonely walk into the village, for after numbering in the thousands three days ago, the lapland longspurs have heard their cue given and have exited en masse and have diminished by one the number of actors in this brief drama of summer's births and deaths, comings and goings. I imagine the birds raised within sight of my tent on this sanctuary hillside in flight on this blustery afternoon, perhaps as far south as the Aleutian Peninsula; perhaps even now within sight of Katmai's volcanic fires. I hope they have tenacity and skill enough to gain passage through the dark skies. The longspurs have left, but with August have come the flowers; the white, lace-like yarrow, the cotton grass, but mostly in variations on a leitmotif of purple have come the monk's hood, the fireweed, and the aster. In purple too, and named for a character in a Dicken's novel, have come the Dolly Varden trout, with August's color speckling their emerald sides. Their cycle in the river has begun as the chum salmon's is ending. Each trip upriver to fish the fly, I step over thousands of chum carcasses, in every imaginable attitude of repose and stage of decomposition. They are draped over underwater limbs and roots and are wedged between stones. Their hoary, eyeless heads nod gently in the current. Some of the expressive faces seem to wear masks of tragedy and some, farce. The sea bright dollies line up behind the chums, reds, and kings still on the spawning beds and feed voraciously on the colorful, translucent eggs. Many of the ones I catch on the fly rod have stomachs full of them, like white pouches of orange and pink pearls. The exhausted and dying fish make no effort to repell these new enemies. The chums still living are "water marked," streaked with purple and black, while the enormous kings, cruelly metamorphized from the handsome silver ocean heavyweights, spend their dwindling energy stores, splotched white where chunks of flesh have fallen away. I wade up behind a dying forty pound king holding in the shallows and roll up my shirt sleeve and grasp him at the base of his tail, as thick as my upper arm, but he does not struggle. The male sockeyes are pathetically hookjawed and hump-backed and both genders are brilliant red; they flash in the clear depths like tongues of underwater flame.

August 5 — Fished this morning among the white caps...

Fished this morning among the whitecaps in worsening weather. Small flocks of black turnstone and western sandpiper flash by the boat as it rocks among the waves at the foot of Big Beluga. After we feed the net over the side of the boat, and watch the one hundred yard cork line snake through the field of whitecaps, my young helper, a sixteen-year-old boy from the village, sleeps in the corner of the cabin, oblivious to the weather, which has my stomach fidgeting with worry. My eyes follow the near vertical walls of this most prominent landmark on Melancholy Bay, pausing to study the knots of gulls and cormorants on the exposed stone. The black cormorants dive from their perches and slide down the twenty knot wind where it boils around the rock faces. The gulls, like random splashes of whitewash on Beluga's face, huddle quietly. Much of Beluga's near vertical face is covered in thick grass. On a windy day like this, it tosses like a Viking's beard; in sunlight it glows like the oxidized dome of a state capitol. William Galila, who grew up at the foot of Beluga when small family units lived year round in dozens of sites around Melancholy Bay, before the school and the village store and the airstrip brought all together, told me of a clash, hundreds of years ago, between a band of roving warriors from the mouth of the Kuskokwim River and the men of Melancholy Bay. According to oral history, the arrows and lances of the Melancholy men killed all the invaders except one who picked and clawed his way up Beluga's apathetic face. I have heard several versions of the story, and in my favorite, the warrior, knowing no one else would try what he had just accomplished, had paused to urinate from the dizzy heights to show his contempt, and then had disappeared over the top in the direction of the Kuskokwim. In those days, all things, from war, fought with quaint, handmade weapons, to insult, were done on a far more personal and sincere level.

A single boat in the endless field of rolling, hissing whitecaps sets his net out a quarter of a mile below us. I know it to be the boat of Robert James, the old man still fishing alone at age sixty-eight. He was raised twenty-five miles up the North Fork of the Melancholy River, in a place where several white crosses stand, and half a dozen sunken pits are swallowed up in high grass. The last time I was there, one of the misanthropic Melancholy bears had just left a set of tracks, each of which dwarfed my outstretched hand. The tiny figure of Robert James throws up his hand in greeting. He knows better than my young Eskimo helper or I know, that great emptiness of space, together with a high wind, make togetherness very sweet.

Later we pull in the net and, with the wind at our backs, riding atop the waves, we "surf" all the way back to the point. Several times, at the bottom of a trough, I bury the nose of the boat into the back of the next wave, much to the delight of my helper who, laughing wildly, bails the salt water out as it runs back to the splash well. The point is empty; the DC-3 that we had heard, finding no hole in the clouds, had circled and left. No fish will be bought this day. We give away our small load of reds, or sockeyes, and chums and a few late kings, to the villagers my young helper calls "the old people." Walking up the hill I am poorer than when I woke up this morning at 4:00 a.m., but somehow I don't feel so.

August 6 — Anchored the boat at the point, where I mop fish...

Anchored the boat at the point, where I mop fish slime and blood
from the deck. Thin cirrus clouds are arranged in endless rows like
the furrows of a heavenly plow. On the shore, Barney drags a small
log, growling at it. His tolling dog behavior attracts many birds.
Northern phalaropes, tree swallows and cliff swallows fly past me
where I stand in the bow of the boat. An arctic tern hovers a few
feet over Barney's head, wings perfect wind scythes, flashing with
stroboscopic rhythm. I can faintly hear them slicing the air. He
flings strange rattling, clicking, porpoise-like cries at the heedless
Barney. While Melancholy Bay is mired in the eighteen hour
nights of winter, this masked sprite will be near Antarctica, exper-
iencing, proportionately, more hours of sunlight in his brief life
than any other living creature.

Finished with my cleaning, I walk up the airstrip toward the
village, hoping fervently for a letter. Light-footed little Ester
Aluskak falls in beside me. In her hip boots, she mocks my heavy
gussack's tread with Brobdignagian steps. She has fished all night
too, in an eighteen foot Lund skiff with no cabin. A single salmon
scale has dried on her left cheek and has become a beauty mark.

On this morning I notice Steve Perkin's super cub, having blown in on some nocturnal wind, is parked by the airstrip. Steve is a mountain man, misplaced in time. He is a puller on a fishing boat in Bristol Bay in the summer, and in the fall seeks gold in the Lake Illiamna area. I am surprised on this day of hot sun to see him walking toward my tent from the village. He knows I have a good camera and explains that he has seen a great and unprecedented gathering of walrus. We leave immediately to get pictures but when the plane sputters briefly, Steve lands on the other side of the bay, on the beach. He drains some gas for each wing tank into his cupped hands and looks closely at it, searching for droplets of water. He flings the gas away and wipes his hands on eelgrass lying on the beach and then dry on his jeans. He lifts the tail wheel out of a pocket of soft sand and places it on the hard, wave packed beach and we drone up and away once again. I watch the oversized balloon tundra tire just beneath my window as it continues to spin rapidly for a few seconds after we have leaped from the ground. We fly at about one hundred feet, as Steve looks out the window for anything interesting. He shouts to me over the engine, "Bear trails!" and points to a small creek below us and ten minutes later, "Seals!" as we fly over a spit of sand. I look where Steve points and see them lying like a litter of basking puppies, silver ones, black ones, spotted ones, dozens of them. They remind me of a cache of jewels, so fetching and exotic are they. I twist around in the tiny seat, trying to treasure up the sight, but I cannot see beyond Barney's august profile. He gazes serenely out the window until he notices my face is turned and deliberately bumps me with his icy nose. In the distance ahead I can see a long, even beach between an inlet and a rocky promontory. It appears to be covered with large boulders from one end to the other, but as the plane nears I can see that it is covered with walrus. Steve turns around and grins at me, "There's more than before; no place to land." But land we do, in the dunes behind the herd, the plane staying down after the third bounce. We crawl walrus-fashion to within fifty feet and sit in the sand, staring in amazement. As far as I can see down the beach is an ocean of pink walrus flesh. I feel as one who looks through a window in time upon a fantasy of pre-history. The sheer mass is hard for me to comprehend, even though I can nearly reach out and touch the closes bull. There is something very human about them, as they take pause during their Odyssian migration. There are flippers over cavernous, yawning mouths, and flippers scratching armpits; the air is full of a cacophony of grunts, thuds, and belches. There are thundered accusations of impropriety, as here there is a tusk in a nearby flank and there a flipper gouges a neighbor's eye. Sporadically, there is a rearing of great heads and a clicking of ivory on ivory. Steve's glazed eyes are those of one who gazes upon the mother lode. Gussacks, or white people, are allowed to collect tusks from dead animals that wash up on the beach, but only Eskimos may hunt them for ivory. Steve whispers to me, "Out of so many, one is bound to die of a heart attack. A set of horns would pay the taxes on my plane for the year." The beach is shrouded with a cloud of steam that rises from the huge bodies as still more bulls haul out to bask in the sun with a fervor that only one who has spent all morning digging up the floor of the dark, icy Bering Sea in search of bivalves many miles offshore, can muster.

The naked, gargantuan hedonism of the huge creatures, so ungainly and absurd on land, but moving with a startling grace and swiftness once in the water, makes me remember what I once read about whales. I had read that whales do everything in a way that is larger than life; that they are days at a time in their singing and love-making, and are prodigious in their love affair with their element. I begin to understand. I have never seen such a riotous celebration of sun worship. Like the heliotropic sunflower, they turn first one part of their anatomy and then another into the sun's rays. The smell of urine is like ammonia; the wind made warm by body heat. Overhead, flocks of kittiwakes, small gulls with wing-tips as if dipped in black ink, wheel as they look for littoral life stirred up by the behemoths.

We are both shocked to see two native skiffs offshore, moving slowly toward the herd. As they idle against the tide, it is as if the handmade wooden boats themselves have eyes that are bulging in wonder at the sight of this extraordinary haul out. Steve and I wait for the first shots and the pandemonium which must come but the boats only rise and fall on the gentle swell. In this attitude Steve and I wait for ten minutes. He begins to laugh softly and then the laugh grows in confidence. The skiffs, as if exorcized by Steve's hearty laugh, turn and leave the walrus to their reverie. "They don't have their guns with them," he says, grinning.

We have alarmed the nearby bulls and dozens surge forward into the sea. Not wanting to disturb the slumber of the rest, we walk back to the plane, where a disgusted, tethered Barney lies in the shadow of one wing. We fly back to Melancholy Bay in silence, each of us lost in thoughts triggered by the rare event we have seen.

August 8 – On this day I am still under the spell of the walrus.

On this day I am still under the spell of the walrus. I have an overpowering urge to return to them; to gaze once again upon their primeval innocence, but Steve's plane, like the swallow that seldom perches for more than a moment, is gone. Outside my tent I sit and stare at the undulating hills that seem to have been momentarily frozen in a northwesterly migration in some forgotten age and, with the image of the walrus herd rushing into the sea, I suddenly know what they remind me of. I remember reading in one of Hemingway's books on Africa that the hills he loved reminded him of elephants in the distance. I decide that my Melancholy hills suggest dinosaurs. Most have the gentle, elongated lines of the great plant-eating brontosaurus, but Beluga suggests a rearing Tyrannosaurus rex, frozen like Lot's wife, but into a pillar of stone, as he took one last look at the sea. And so I see my hills differently now, as if I alone, because of the key given to my imagination by the walrus, know their true identity. In summer, their living green mass seems to me to move in subliminal respiration; in fall they turn to gold, and then to brown, and seem to lower their heads as their old enemies, ice and snow, begin to cover them. Just as ontogeny recapitulates phylogeny, so does the passing year summarize the Mesozoic Era, bringing my hillsides to life, covering them briefly in green, and then stinging them with death. And I alone watch their doomed cycle and my heart goes out to them.

August 9 – This morning a family group of young, yellow wagtails...

This morning a family group of young, yellow wagtails has discovered that the sloping roof of my tent is a fine place for walking. From where we sit inside, Barney watches the shadowy, moving forms on the roof intently. He bumps the wall of the tent with his nose to scare them off. He lies, staring at the outline of a sock which I put on the roof to dry, thinking it to be a stubborn bird. The look of affront on his face clearly says, "How dare he!"

August 10 – Went upriver to the Alaska Department of Fish and Game's salmon counting tower...

Went upriver to the Alaska Department of Fish and Game's salmon counting tower so I could talk to someone. Sat on the tower with my friend Harry, watching the reds, chums, and occasional kings as they dart across the white, plywood panels held in place by sandbags on the bottom of the river, spanning the entire channel. A few fish dart across the panels without hesitation, but most hang nervously behind the strange barrier, then flit quickly over it and continue upstream. Harry's counter clicks rapidly, tallying the fish. Even up in the tower where there is a constant breeze, the bugs are fierce. Camped overnight and floated out without using the motor, fishing the most inviting pools and riffles. Drifting downstream, casting to the undercut bank, the three pound rainbows flash pink when they turn while taking the fly. Barney groans loudly as boat, man, dog, and the fish being played on the fly rod, all sweep past the willows on the shore. I take the fly from their mouths without lifting them from the water. Their broad sides look as if sprinkled with coarse ground pepper. The pink stripe, startling in its brightness, is the last color I see as the released fish swims back into the shadowy depths.

As I drift out I stop to fish the backwaters, ponds, and oxbows where the first silver salmon in the river stop to rest as they move upstream to spawn. They cruise slowly with their dorsal fins cutting the surface. While they take spoons and other lures more readily than flies, they will take colorful streamers and bucktails, and I am always glad to see them back in the river, for they are the most sporting of the Pacific salmon. Bringing one in on a light fly rod is arm tiring work, and not nearly as interesting as fishing the riffles and runs for trout. For Barney, getting one to the shore is more of a brawl than a clean retrieve.

August 12 – Already there are signs of fall,

Already there are signs of fall, both in new appearances and in departures of old friends. Flocks of whimbrels, so like the curlew with their downward curved, scythe-like bills, land on the tundra near my tent to eat crowberries. When they spring into the air, the flock seems not so much two dozen birds, as it does two dozen mirrored images on one bird, so perfectly in time are the wingbeats. Emperor geese and lesser Canadian geese have drifted in, as well as the tiny, goldfinch-like redpoll, but the hillside around my tent is conspicuously silent each morning for the white crowned and golden crowned sparrows, the thicket minstrels, have left. The purple flowers are nearly gone, as are the swallows. The yellow warblers and Wilson's warblers, to the alder bushes what the tiny flecks of gold dust are to the swirling gravel of the miner's pan, are also gone. The predominant bird that I see each day is the savanna sparrow. Among the smallest and most frail of the songbirds, the gusts of wind buffet them cruelly as they forage about. Do they stay to savor the willows as their exclusive domain now that the larger, more aggressive birds have left, or do they linger in dread of the endless journey that lies before them? They dally week after week, unconcerned as Barney, as the air loses its smell of seaweed and salt and takes on the sharp and stony smell of fall, whenever the wind blows out of the north.

The old ladies of the village, many in their sixties and seventies, wander far from the village with their berry scoops and buckets. I encounter them miles from the village on my solitary walks with Barney. They are frightened when they see a man, and they are so far from the village. When they recognize us they laugh, sounding so much like the cackle of ptarmigan that I laugh back in wonderment.

64

August 13 – Rain falls softly on the roof of my tent,

Rain falls softly on the roof of my tent, as it has so consistently all summer. I wonder, has the sun forsaken the entire earth, or just Melancholy Bay? The dreary gray sky, the heavy rain clouds rolling in from the southeast, make me feel like I could never face another summer like this one. Through the tent flaps I look longingly up the valley of the Melancholy River where a shaft of sunlight plays. Finding a hole in the endless gray ceiling, it shines through, creating a vignette of a tiny, sunlit world. The hole closes quickly and it vanishes.

August 14 – After a slow start, good numbers of silver, or coho, salmon...

After a slow start, good numbers of silver, or coho, salmon are coming into the bay. When the water is not dirty after rough weather, they can see the net and many of them avoid it. Several times today I saw individuals jump over the cork line of the net. It makes me sad to be killing such a noble fish, only trying to get up-river to spawn. Still, harvesting part of the run is biologically sound, for if all returning fish were allowed to go upriver to spawn, there would be much waste, since newly arriving salmon would destroy previously made redds containing fertilized eggs, to deposit their own. The fluctuating water level takes its toll too. Often, eggs deposited during June's high water are left high and dry by September. Those who spend hundreds of hours immersed in nature each year, know her scheme to be extravagant, capricious, and routinely murderous; placing little value on the life of the individual of any species. The numbers go up and down wildly. Dan tells me that on his sled dog trips two springs ago, the ptarmigan rose before his sled in countless flocks of hundreds. This past spring in the same traditional winter range area, there were practically none. It would seem that the ideals of tranquility and mercy exist only in the mind of Man.

> "Sow the seed generously
> one for the rook, one for the crow
> one to die, and one to grow."
> *old nursery rhyme*

The yin and yang inherent in every facet of life in Melancholy Bay becomes more and more easy for me to accept. Having been well schooled in Paradise Lost's good versus evil and subtle Calvinism, I am gently disabused by my new mentor.

On this day I work not with my hands, but with my brain, something I ordinarily avoid while on Melancholy Bay for the summer. In this summer of weak salmon prices I have become a temporary partner in fish buying with a gussack who lives at the opposite end of the bay in the tiny village of Ruby. A few boats from "my" end of the bay pull in to sell and they are surprised to see me adding figures on a calculator and weighing fish. One of my native friends tells me, "I lost you at our end of the bay," meaning he missed me.

Fish buying is not what I come to Melancholy Bay to do, and I am sure this is only temporary, but it has revealed to me another level of logistical thinking within the sphere of salmon fishing. As a fisherman I only have to figure on wind, tide and fish, but now the buyer in Dillingham must be called and told which plane to send; the DC-3, the "Ag truck," or the Single Engine Otter, and how many fish are likely to come out of the bay on this opening. A falling ceiling means that I must pull in my net and go to the village to call the buyer with the news that he has one hour to get his plane in. Getting out is his problem. I feel like Mark Twain, who as a boy had regarded the shoals, the snags, the storm clouds above the Mississippi River as things of beauty; and as liabilities as a paddlewheeler pilot. It is a game of percentages and always the success of the operation rides on the courage and skill of the pilots. My favorite is Bo Darden, who flies the Single Engine Otter. Bo owns his plane and is paid by the poundage that he flies out. The Otter has the lines of a World War II aircraft and the Eskimos sometimes make remarks to the effect that it looks like a duck, which seems to me that it should be a compliment, except I think they mean a sitting, rather than a flying, duck. The insult of an Eskimo is usually well thought out, and these remarks usually earn a stern look from Bo, who loves his plane as I love my lowsided, underpowered, unbelievably heavy, boat. When I met Bo, I knew instantly from his accent, but even more by his droll, unhurried way, that he was from North Carolina and when he drops out of the clouds, if it is possible for an engine to have a drawl, his does.

During the last period, there was gravel under one end of the balance scale and the scales underweighed by about twenty percent. At the end of the day, Mike, for whom I am working, noticed that the four plane loads should have weighed a lot more than the tally sheet showed. I stood on the scales and was recorded at 170 pounds; a weight I will never see again while alive. That night we went to the two dozen houses in the village of Ruby and gave the fishermen an envelope containing the money they had coming. Each man, with his family, sat before a snowy T.V. screen.

Many times during those weeks in August as a fish buyer, operating at both ends of the bay, I would help Bo load the last tubs of iced salmon, watch him climb into the cockpit of his plane, give me thumbs up and then fly off into the descending fog and mist, the sound of his slow stroking engine lingering long after he himself had been swallowed up by the deepening gloom. Walking back to Mike's shack where I was staying, I would imagine him behind the glowing controls, mouth in a tight line, flying through the rocky corridors behind here and Dillingham.

August 16 – Inspired by the breaking up of rain clouds,

Inspired by the breaking up of rain clouds, went upriver for the weekend. Making camp, I discovered that one of the eighteen inch fiberglass tent rods that gives the umbrella tent its support, was missing. Taped the tip section of my fly rod where the missing piece belonged. Speculating on my handiwork, I reflected on the time when I had forsaken the fly reel for the spinning reel. When I had first come to Alaska, I learned that the heavy current required using lead shot to put the fly in front of trout where they lay in the river's depths. During a cast, the wind caused the weighted flies to behave unpredictably as they neared the vicinity of my naked ears. Three large split shot sinkers pack a surprising amount of energy when they strike the rear of the caster's head, as they rebound from a mighty backcast. So rather than duck the whizzing lead shot and the evil, barbed hooks, I attached a closed face spinning reel to the seat of my fly rod. I found I could fling a cast of weighted flies with an ease that was exhilerating. I found I could present the flies in the deepest pools without the worry of a dragging fly line. I could cast twice the distance, without any backcast, and I caught fish; but not more than a dozen before I realized I was robbing myself.

I missed watching the fly line serenely floating on the broad back of the current, seeing it instantly spring to life when a fish took the fly on the end of the eight foot leader. I missed the electric sound of a braking fly reel when a new, unseen fish runs and I wonder how it is that any sound could be so filled with promise. But mostly I missed the sensation. Catching a fish on spinning tackle, one only has the rod to transfer the feel of the fish in the current, and worse still, many of the fish are too deeply hooked to be released. With the balanced fly rod and reel, it is as if the thick, tactile fly line is an elongated nerve that telegraphs the nervous clicking and chattering and tapping as the flies dribble their way through dark, fish holding water, occasionally touching bottom. It is as if the hypnotic inner spirit of the river flows, in a low voltage stream of sensations into my brain through the fly line. When a fish takes the fly, the long, arching fly rod, the singing reel, the strumming fly line, all come together to create an experience that pulls the fly fisherman far from hearth and home in pursuit of his sport.

And so I cast the fly, and when the wind blows, I duck.

August 19 - Anticipating that I will soon be leaving the land...

Anticipating that I will soon be leaving the land of the salmon, I now relish what I have been taking for granted all summer. I look closely at the orange flesh that springs open like a cantalope when I clean a large female fish. The two skeins of eggs fill both my hands. I first boil them until they are leathery and then fry them in oil. I eat them on Pilot Bread, a thick unsalted cracker that I see only in Alaska, but which is baked in Richmond, Virginia. I filet out the slabs of orange flesh, being careful to leave the ribs behind. I fry it or poach it in a quarter inch of water after browning and eat it with rice, or, more commonly, alone, with a little mayonnaise on the side. Early in the season I eat salmon without condiments, but by July I have grown tired of it alone. I learned of mayonnaise with salmon from Number Two Bob, who works on Mike's boat at the other end of the bay. He tells people that the fish he most identifies with is the number two chum salmon. The chum or dog salmon, is the least prized of all the salmon, and a number two chum is so designated because it is beginning to turn soft; most fish buyers won't take them. Sometimes, when the wind isn't blowing I can hear Bob's harmonica and wailing blues voice coming from Mike's boat singing, "Don't give me none of them number two chums." And all of us; small time, leaky boat fishermen who won't make in a season what the big thirty-two foot diesel gillnetters make in a week on Bristol Bay, smile and listen, and feel better.

Last season the captain Bob fished with in Bristol Bay left town without paying Bob his season's percentage. He is now one of us, a Melancholy lost soul. He lives in Ruby in the most pathetic shack in the village, a discarded salmon net mesh draped elegantly over the entrance. On the unpainted plywood walls inside are powerful and moving felt tip pen drawings of everything from saber tooth tigers to outboard motors. He makes his winter wages in San Diego, selling sketches of passersby in the public parks. It is well known that Number Two Bob will do a drawing for free, will sing and play his harmonica for a place at the table, can easily be deceived; and is welcome in any household on the bay, either Eskimo or gussack.

August 20 — The gnats seem to peak with the silvers...

The gnats seem to peak with the silvers and this is an exceptional year for both. Clear, windy days are a blessing. I sit outside the tent and watch the marsh hawks ride the thermals that rise along my hillside. In the distance, sandhill cranes spiral dizzily out of sight, even though their rachetting call sounds deceivingly close. The raven, master of voices, mimic of gong and chime, flies over my camp, answering my imperfect imitation of his call with silence, foregoing even his usual perfunctory sideways glance at my tent, so great is his contempt for this creature that cannot spread his wings and fly over the mountain, cannot stand the winter cold, becomes lonely within a few hours of being left alone, cannot even dong like the chapel bell in the village church.

Anxious to have as many days and nights on the river as possible
before leaving for the year, went up for the weekend again. By now
the river is down considerably from its June level and one must
read it very carefully for the channel is the only place deep enough
to allow passage by propeller. I avoid the gravel bars that hide
under several inches of water. I do this subconsciously, for I am
thinking of a conversation I had with Robert James yesterday. In
the old days, he told me, the men in kayaks went upriver, against
even June's swift freshet by propelling themselves upstream with a
pair of smooth four foot sticks, the diameter of a broom handle. He
showed me the motion used with the sticks; his arms moving
rapidly in unison, like a skier pushing off from a standstill. "We
could go many miles upriver in a single day" he told me. "We
carried a paddle for the trip down." When Robert talks of the
kayaks that he made by hand many years ago, he becomes quite
excited; his deeply lined, leathery face becomes twenty-five years
younger. "They were good. We go everywhere. Cross the bay
against the tide, against the wind. Go all the way upriver to
Melancholy Lake. Sleep in it at night. Hunt seals in it." "Why
don't you use one now, instead of your skiff and outboard motor?" I
ask him. "Too slow," he tells me. "What's the hurry?" I ask. "You
brought the hurry," he says, a forgiving smile on his face.

I turn into a sharp bend and watch the wake wash heavily into
the bank as Barney moves to the opposite side of the front seat to
balance the speeding skiff. In my mind is a vision of a man in a
kayak making this very turn, only powered by two polished sticks
and the muscles of his arms and back. I stop at the grave sites
where Robert James was born and tie the anchor rope to a willow. I
walk to the overlook and stand facing into the wind that rises off
the river. Only my face is vulnerable to the fierce gnats and when I
turn so that the light wind is at my back and my face is not washed
by its current, I am instantly bitten savagely. I turn quickly into the

river wind again. Barney watches the pool fifty feet below us where a dozen sockeye salmon revolve slowly with the clockwise current in an eddy along the bank. His short tail ticks back and forth like a metronome.

I walk back down to the boat and put the fly rod together and begin to fish the long run at the foot of the pool below the dropoff. I know this is primarily Dolly Varden water, rather than rainbow, so I tie on a pair of "bargain flies," since the dollies are not particular. Bargain flies are flies that are falling apart after numerous maulings by large trout. Often the yarn bodies are partly unravelled and the hooks dulled to nubs after many sharpenings. I do not care if some of the dollies get off since I release most of them anyway; the strike is the thing. I am occupied in this manner, with Barney at my side when Otto Wassilie, who speaks no English, comes upriver and seeing the eccentric gussack who catches fish on a rod and reel where he uses a gill net, pulls up to watch. I catch several trout and throw them into Otto's boat, which pleases him immensely. Even though we share not a single common word in our two vocabularies, we have no difficulty in communicating that this is a good way to get fish, that Barney is an extraordinary fisherman, and that, in general, it is a good day to be alive and on the Melancholy. I show him by fly boxes and he holds up the various patterns, telling me in Yupik, that he must learn to tie his own; I think. On this note of concord and unanimity, Otto pull starts his outboard motor and heads upriver and is nearly out of sight around the bend when we both notice that Barney is standing in the front of his boat, ears planed off in the wind, looking for fish in the shallows. Otto delivers Barney to me and we both laugh and shake our heads and then gravely shake hands to commemorate the absurdity of the event.

I float out that evening in the dusk back to camp without the motor. The water dripping from the paddle, the sounds of the river, are a powerful soporific. I imagine Robert James paddling down this stretch of the river in a kayak, half a century ago.

August 25 – On this cloudy, windy day, walked to the rock fields ...

On this cloudy, windy day, walked to the rock fields along the
spine of the ridge that rises five hundred feet above my tent. All
soil has been scoured from this place. The small boulders and rocks
are colored, textured and patterned like the copperhead, the anaconda, and the diamondback. This is a different habitat than the
alpine tundra with pockets of alder which stops abruptly several
hundred feet below me. The snow bunting claims this angular, dis-
heveled rooftop of the world as his own. A flock feeds ahead of me
among the stones and their faint, chipping calls are carried past
my ears like tiny, windborne ice crystals. I once watched a young
Peregrine falcon, a bird of the year, chase a flock of ptarmigan
down this ridge in a wild free-for-all. Avian predation is an
extravagant way to make a living and the young bird was
learning that the cost of his ferocious temperment was high
in calories and disappointment.

    The sun illuminates a jumble of ridges and valleys to the
northeast and I glass the area with my binoculars. The green of life
extends searching fingers up the valley walls into the rocky faces,
among the snowbanks. Where it can find one tiny bit of dirt, some
form of greenery will claim it. Beyond the highlighted pocket, unnamed mountains recede into the gray distance like rows of shark's
teeth. From the next ridge to the north, the hoarse call of the
raven carries with remarkable tenacity and clarity. His call is one of
the few sounds one hears in this landscape in winter when it becomes utterly forbidding to most warm-blooded forms of life. Like a
bizarre jester, he mindlessly plays before a court turned to stone.

In this gray and sunless time of winter's purgatory, life's ebbing pulse becomes thin and faint. From the village, surrounded by the apathetic backs of mountains cloaked in dull silver, comes the crack of a twenty-two caliber rifle, and an hour later, the muted tolling of the chapel bell. Another poor soul has thrown the spinning wheel of fortune from his back.

Life flickers like St. Elmo's fire on this earth, here for a moment and then gone for a time; as fickle and capricious as the interest of a child.

August 26 – It is a great comfort to see the Big Dipper...

It is a great comfort to see the Big Dipper hanging directly over my tent. I know that in just over a month I will be gazing at it from the Canadian prairies where Barney and I will hunt sharptail grouse along the yellow grain fields where the crickets sing on the hillsides and the sun shines nearly every day. I look about my tent at the familiar folding table and single chair, the Coleman cook stove, the paperback books whose characters have been my companions and friends for another summer. The tent is littered with empty powdered milk envelopes and crumpled pieces of wet newspaper that I have stuffed into my hip boots after each fishing period to dry them out. The tent is a depressing mess, but I do nothing about it. As long as the lantern gives me light to read and write by, and the stove will cook salmon, everything else is overlooked. I have gone nearly two months since last bathing thoroughly. While that may sound abominable, it is not. The body has its own means of keeping itself clean. I do not smell any stronger than I did after the first week. While it is necessary to brush the teeth daily and change the underwear and socks regularly, the rest does not matter, within reason. All superflous activity ceased a month ago. Barney gives the dishes their only washing when he licks them clean. I check any salmon or char I cook for him as carefully as I do my own, for tapeworms. While my body is wonderfully healthy and fit, I pine for companionship. I daydream of highways that make traveling easy and of grocery stores with bins of fresh fruit and vegetables, and of the sight of women in dresses.

August 27– Wonderful fishing lately.

Wonderful fishing lately. All five of the "Melancholy factors:" good fishing weather, not too calm and not too rough, the condition of the net, not too many unmended holes and tears, the condition of the engines, price per pound, and the presence of a buyer, are all lined up in my favor for the first time this season. I know one or more of the "factors" will turn on me soon, but with luck I will have made the season pay by then. The last three commercial periods I had good loads. Strained my back carrying a thirty-five horse outboard motor up the beach. Pulling in the net seems to loosen it up. Had to fill the cabin with silvers last period to get more weight to the rear of the boat. Each period we catch a few salmon which have defective biological time clocks. Instead of first spawning upriver and then degenerating, these fish have aged prematurely while still in salt water. When I lift the female fish from the net to throw them over the side, the pink eggs dribble out in a stream onto the deck. Upriver, the shallows are filled with dying and rotting sockeyes, even as the fresh silvers stream in. On the sandbars, salmon skeletons, masterpieces of design, whiten in the sun.

August 30 – On this weekend I took my boat,

On this weekend I took my boat, towing the sixteen foot skiff behind, twenty miles down the coast to do some exploring. Left the shelter of Melancholy Bay with nothing more than a stiff breeze and a gentle, rocking swell on the ocean. Halfway there, off Roan Mountain, the swell had turned into angry six foot seas and by the time I was in sight of Ahklun Bay, the seas had frothy whitecaps and the skiff kept surfing down the faces of them, until it was even with me in the big boat, nearly ramming me repeatedly. Several times it nearly swamped and I was afraid I would have to cut it loose. I pulled into the mouth of Ahklun Bay and anchored the boat in a place where the Eskimos lived continuously since the time of Christ, until a few decades ago, when most of the family groups moved to the village of Melancholy Bay. Now the only signs of human habitation are the mounds and depressions which create a series of parallel forms, made by generations of Eskimos as the shoreline retreated during the last two thousand years. It is late afternoon and I walk through the tall grass which always heralds ancient village sites due to the enriching debris left behind by Man. As always, there are clam shells on the beach. I was told by a native friend that the old people always like to have clams to fall back on, if the other food sources all failed. One of the mounds is used by the hunters of Melancholy Bay as a camp when they come here in the spring to hunt geese as they return to nest. Between the other depressions are well worn bear trails and before I step into them, I depend on Barney to tell me if they are occupied. The abundant bear dung contains digested parka squirrels, fish scales and bones, and grass.

Walking through the tall, wind tossed grass, I stoop to pick up what appears to be one of the most common artifacts, a piece of a bowl made of mud, dog hair and dried blood. It is the top of a human skull, with light green moss growing inside the braincase. I carefully put it back in its place. I remember that Charlie Toniak, who spent part of his youth here before the last families moved to the villages of Ruby and Melancholy Bay, told me that the rocky cliffs in the next bay down the coast, Snug Cove, have ghostly voices.

I return to my boat, anchored in front of the village site, and stand on the gently rolling deck as the moon rises over the jagged rocks which seem to form Tolkeinesque fortresses in the transforming half light. I try to imagine this place with dozens of kayaks pulled out beyond the reach of the high tide, wood smoke rising in thin lines, and with the sound of laughter and the thump of the hand-held skin drum, as it was during the days of the Roman Empire, the Norse invasions of Europe, the Dark Ages, through the rule of Charlemagne, the Renaissance, the discovery of the New World, through World War I. The place seems to be in mourning.

The next day I take the boat another five miles down the coast to Snug Cove. The north wind has given me a completely blue sky and so I set off on a day's walk. At noon I have reached the other side of Cape Nelson and I am surprised to learn that I can see the place of the walrus from here. I glass it with my binoculars, and even though it is several miles away, I can see that they have left. I sit near the edge of a sheer three hundred foot drop off and eat some crowberries that I have gathered. Barney and I nap for half an hour in the sun and as I rise to begin the walk across the cape to Snug Cove, I am surprised to hear voices. I know no boat would anchor off such a rocky beach, but so sure am I that I heard voices that I glass the entire beach, seeing nothing. As I stand there, the sound comes unmistakably now, sounding so much like babies at play in a crib that chills tingle in the back of my neck. I think of Charlie and his superstitions. Surely it is the voice of the cormorant, or the murre of the puffin which I see below, on the rocky outcroppings. And yet I notice that I am quite cold and feel it is a good time to begin the walk back to the boat.

It is nearly dark when I reach the boat and Snug Cove is glassy calm. I cook a piece of salmon, but am strangely restless, and remembering the ride down, decide I will make a night voyage home, before the wind-pumping sun rises. I make it out of the mouth of Snug Cove just as the first stars appear and I find the north star after locating the Big Dipper, and head in the direction of Melancholy Bay. Soon the moon is on my right shoulder and I run with it as a companion for several hours, until I can see the tiny lights of Ruby near the entrance to Melancholy Bay. As I run up the coastline, I think of the night I went to the houses of the Ruby fishermen to give them the money Mike and I owed them. Surely among the households, I looked upon many of the great grandchildren of him whose skull I picked up yesterday. I look over my shoulder at the mouth of deserted Ahklun Bay, where the silhouettes of the mountains slope to the sea, and think of the Ruby people, probably even now staring at their snowy T.V. screens.

It is a Saturday night and someone has walked to the beach behind Ruby and fired a roman candle into the sky. The single, tiny, soundless puff of red and green sparks is instantly swallowed up by the vastness of the night, but no more eloquent statement could have been made that even though Ahklun Bay is dark and deserted, this coastline still supports that most unpredictable life form; Man.

September 10 – A necrosis has begun to appear, patches of dull gold in the ocean of green grass...

A necrosis has begun to appear, patches of dull gold in the ocean of green grass in the river's flood plain. A few yellow leaves have appeared on the willows. The alders are later to turn. Nearly all the song birds have left, I am feeling an atavistic restlessness; a need to face challenges and win passage. Does the swan, as she waits on a tundra pond, fret and decide, and then hesitate again, or does she, on the turning of a moment, know that now is the time to reach for the southern horizon?

September 14 – The run of silvers has nearly ended.

The run of silvers has nearly ended. Many of the twenty-two boat "fleet" of Melancholy Bay have been pulled up on the beach for the winter. Last period I caught only ten salmon. My helper has returned to high school and I fish alone. I walk to the boat, the stars bright overhead at 4:00 a.m. The boat is rimed with ice. I make long drifts since fish hit the net only occasionally.

I watch flocks of migrating ducks, geese, and shorebirds, resting in Melancholy Bay as they move down the coastline. A flock of thousands of tiny dunlin and sandpipers, changing directions as one entity, flashes against the background of the Irish-looking hills, like a momentary puff of white smoke. Throughout the entire avian community, body fat stores and length of day have made the air pregnant with urgency.

September 17 — Went upriver for what may be the last time...

Went upriver for what may be the last time this summer; the river so low that the propeller found the gravel bottom in new and unexpected places. I pull the skiff, loaded with gear, through several riffles too shallow to use the engine. Since bear tracks are on many of the sandbars, the loaded rifle is never far from me while I fish. I wade upstream, using the more subtle patterns in my fly boxes in September's low water, and dead drift the nymph back to me. The big rainbows are in a feeding frenzy, for they sense fall in the air. Even two pound fish strip my line down to the backing. Barney seems to be in a frenzy too. Even when I stop to rest or cook lunch, he continues alone, dragging out the chums and silvers that splash in the riffle near the tent. I throw them back into the river one after another.

I have always thought how remarkable it is that a smell or a sound can transport one across many years to an associated event or place. So it is that today, each time my fly reel, given to me by my father when I was sixteen, races as a fish makes its run, I am carried twenty years back to the Smith River, where my most memorable boyhood hours were spent with my friend, Steve. We two evolved from pragmatic teenage fishermen who followed the hatchery truck which released easily caught, pen raised trout, to seekers of the naturally reproducing, wild brown trout of the Smith's less accessible reaches; and finally into serious fly fishermen. Even today when I cannot relax and fall asleep, the river I fish in my mind's eye as I lie in bed is not the Melancholy, with its hordes of wild rainbows and salmon, nor Montana's blue ribbon streams that I fished through my twenties; it is that humble little tailwater, the Smith River of Virginia. Steve and I, as we progressed in fly fishing sophistication, began to trim with nail clippers the lateral fins of the brown trout we caught and released on our handtied flies, so we could recognize them. We knew where each fish lay, and since their numbers were limited, each one was approached with an anticipation that I have never known since.

Now, each time my fly reel races, I take the wild, Alaskan rainbow with me across twenty years to the Smith River, and I play this one out in the deep hole along the railroad tracks where the river makes the big bend, where Steve and I would sit at dusk and watch the mayflies rise from the river against the rhododendron and laurel. And the next one I might tire under the great sycamore tree in the backyard of the charming, dirty-faced children who Steve and I called "the river urchins." And while I splash through the shallows of the Melancholy toward my tent on a gravel bar, I might imagine jumping a slow moving freight train and riding on the rungs of the steel ladder, holding on with one hand, holding my fly rod in the other, back to where Steve and I always parked.

In the Smith River days, Steve and I made a covenant; that if one of us ever became rich or lived in great trout fishing country, that the other would be his guest each summer for a week's fishing. I chose the road less traveled and, while I am rich only in the sense of owning my time, I have come to know the rivers I dreamed about. Steve has had children and has done well in his profession. I call him long distance from Melancholy Bay and ask him to come, but he can never get away. I can hear his wife and two boys in the background. I walk up the hill alone, wondering what I have become, and what I have given up to live out my dreams. I wonder too, if, just as the swallow lives as she must, and the raven lives as he must, there is really any such thing as free will.

September 23 — Sitting in a light rainfall on this, my birthday...

Sitting in a light rainfall on this, my birthday and my last day in Melancholy Bay for the summer, I have to admire the consistency of this place. In keeping with a season that began with unceasing rain and engine problems, I once again sit on a tarp that covers my duffle bags, hoping desperately again, but this time that the mail plane will make it down to the coast through the endless scud that shrouds the entire southwest coast of Alaska. I have stored my three outboards for the winter, each broken down with similar problems to last year at this time. In the yin-yang of this place it seems that one never really gets ahead, that the caprice of nature and the limitation of man's machinery and wisdom, dictate that Melancholy Bay will ever be true to its name. I have spent myself; have lived with uncertainty as my partner the summer long and am beyond caring. I have kept my covenant with the birds, have fought my personal demons as they fought theirs. I look longingly toward the blue line that is the southern horizon.

September 24 – This day finds Barney and me fifty miles south...

This day finds Barney and me fifty miles south of Anchorage, at
Portage, where we are visiting Harry, who spent the summer on the
Melancholy River salmon counting tower. Harry has advised me
that by taking the train to Whittier one can have a close look at a
glacier. At the railroad siding, where hundreds of dead trees serve
as a reminder to the force of the '64 quake which dropped the entire floor of the valley, I put Barney on a leash and board the train,
explaining to the conductor that we want to get off at the pass that
leads to Portage Glacier from the east. After stepping off the train
and leaving the other passengers wondering what they are missing,
we spend several hours hiking through a terrain so different from
the bleakness of Melancholy Bay, that I cannot walk more than
fifty yards without stopping to take pictures. Having spent the
summer in a part of the state that is below the tree line that snakes
through southwest Alaska just to the north of Melancholy Bay, I
am used to being able to see over the dwarf willows and alder
bushes of the tundra. I examine the trunk of a large spruce, studying the fascinating texture and color of its bark, the thickness and
strength of the trunk at the base as if seeing one for the first time.
Barney and I continue to climb until we stand at the edge of what
could pass as a walkway for the gods as they descend from Olym-
pus. A river of heavy, cold air flows down the steep face of the
glacier. From a distance, it looks like a highway, complete with
center line, but standing here, the chunks of ice are huge and
jagged, separated by deep chasms, pushing along enormous quantities of crushed rock and dirt. This creeping river of bluish ice
seems like a conduit into the past, when all the world moved more
slowly. I sit at the edge of the ice field, drinking in the cold,
ancient smell, feeling as fleeting and evanescent as the butterfly
whose life is measured in weeks.

Barney and I, in order to catch the train which departs from Whittier, begin our hike back down the pass. An hour later as we walked through the spruce forest, the world I thought I knew turned dissembler; the rock and soil I stood on heaved up as Melancholy Bay's angry swell; the venerable spruce trees reeled like drunken men. I fell to my knees to keep from falling on my face. From the glacier came a deep, rumbling, shuttering boom, as if it had wakened momentarily from its sleep to acknowledge the true reality, of which we see only shadows. Even as I assured myself that it had not happened, the earth and rock under my feet heaved and rolled like the ocean again, and then stood still. I put my arm around the closest spruce like it was in intransigent lover, and then feverishly touched everything around me to see if once again wood and rock were hard and steadfast and not protean fluid as they had been moments ago. Once again the nearby stream tinkled innocently in its stony bed, the clouds floated past overhead, and Barney sniffed unconcernedly up and down a fallen log.

I gingerly walked the remaining miles into Whittier, wondering if, like the world of Alice in Wonderland, things here are not as they actually seem. Traveling through the tunnels and up the valley toward Portage, we were a quiet and thoughtful group of passengers.

September 25 – On this day drove the car I have borrowed...

On this day drove the car I have borrowed from Harry, which is loaded with food, tent, and sleeping bag to Portage Lake where a southeast wind has blown large bergs against the shoreline. I chop off an ice chest full of chips, looking closely at the color of this ice that was formed during the days of the Roman Empire. The steering wheel in my hands feels odd, and it seems strange that a ritualized part of travel, the wheelbarrowing of several tanks of outboard motor gas to the point, where I anchored my boat, is no longer necessary. North of Anchorage, stopped to walk Barney and talked to a fisherman who proudly showed me several small trout he had caught during a morning's fishing. I hadn't the heart to tell him of the Melancholy's wild rainbows.

After driving through the Talkeetna Mountains and the Susitna River drainage, I begin to see high tundra, more colorful than the Melancholy's treeless sea level expanse. Here the openness is broken by "taiga," a Russian word meaning "land of little sticks," creating a landscape that is peppered with stunted black and white spruce and the stately paper birch. As night comes I arrive at the McKinley Park facilities, where I take a "room" in one of the railroad sleeper cars that are permanently parked there.

September 26 – On this day Barney and I set out...

On this day Barney and I set out early to drive to Wonder Lake, during this time when the park shuttle buses are still and private vehicles are allowed. I drive gradually upward, into the heart of this country of unparalleled elegance, feeling as though I am in a living Cezanne or Van Gogh. Each day spent rambling these hills that have turned to the color of rust, where the miniaturized, random highland willows glow, is a promise of sights to be treasured up for a lifetime. The park, with its delicate colors, its tiny, ancient willows, its timeless stillness, is like a vast and holy bonsai garden.

Today Barney and I discover that this has been a good blueberry year in this part of the state. They hang in clusters on every blueberry bush, sweetened and softened by last week's freeze. Barney is a veteran browser of berries, for each summer he picks over the crop of crowberries in the vicinity of my tent so thoroughly that in August, the Eskimo women with their pails do not bother to come there. This morning we are like Hansel and Gretel as we graze along, each of us keeping a competitive, sharp eye out for the bushes most heavily laden. Coming from Melancholy Bay where blueberries do not grow well, I am in a panic that they will be wasted; our appetite for the sweet berries is gargantuan. An hour later, my fingers stained purple, I give up, seeing that we have only picked an area of twenty square yards, on the southfacing slope of one hill among ten thousand hillsides that glow wine red in a park larger than the state of Massachusetts. I sit back on the soft tundra and do the only thing one can do; watch it all go by.

Continuing our way into the park's interior, we drive across the Toklat River which is so young that it has no permanent channel yet, only braids whose fishless waters contain silt and powdered rock. Signs warn that due to heavy bear activity, no walking is allowed in this area. We continue to drive into the afternoon until we have reached Wonder Lake, where we see that Mt. Denali, "The High One" which makes its own weather, has "gone in." As I stand on a hill overlooking Wonder Lake, I watch several spectral white Dall sheep as they move across the canvas of fall color. As the sun slips behind the Alaska Range, a red fox, hunting his way along a snow bank for voles, passes within thirty feet of where we stand motionless.

I drive slowly out of this valley of suspended time, which like "the rose that wastes its fragrance on the desert air" saves its most ephemeral beauty until it is nearly empty of people.

September 27 – Drove east from the Park, down the gravel...

Drove east from the Park, down the gravel Denali Highway, stopping to eat more blueberries. On one such stop, saw fresh droppings of willow ptarmigan. I walk back to the car and load Harry's 16 gauge shotgun and return and begin to seek the grouse-like birds. Barney skirts the edges of the willow thickets, going in when he picks up the scent where the birds have fed early this morning. As the birds spring into the air in their fall plumage, their white wings trigger the image of huge, fluttering moths as they move across this vastness of rust and gold. In spring they will taste bitter after feeding on willow twigs all winter, but while they feed on berries, they are at their best as a table bird. Even though this is our first day of hunting this year, Barney works closely and thoroughly. After nine hunting seasons, he recognizes the habitat and cover that may hold game and only occasionally looks to me for hand signals. In three hours of difficult walking on the spongy, uneven tundra, we find two groups of birds, out of which I kill three ptarmigan.

September 28 – At Tok Junction, headed south,

At Tok Junction, headed south, but not before I stopped and took a long look down the Alaska Highway, remembering the trip Barney and I had made four years ago as we drove up from Montana in my Volkswagen camper to the teaching job where I had first come to know the youths of Melancholy Bay. Frequently I see the silver gleam of the Alaska Pipeline snaking endlessly through the stunted spruce of interior Alaska, opening briefly into deciduous forest as we move south.

September 29—Drove the car onto the ferry at Valdez

Drove the car onto the ferry at Valdez. Feels nice to be on water again, but how different from Melancholy Bay is Prince William Sound. I watch the water's edge for black bear and sitka black-tailed deer. As we near the Columbia Glacier, three dolphins appear off the stern of the ferry and follow alongside our wake for fifteen minutes. Here the salmon season is still in progress and I study the location of set nets as we pass through the dark green, heavily forested islands. We pass a kayaker, riding the incoming tide toward Whittier. I observe him through my binoculars as he dips soundlessly through the islands and fjords.

At Whittier, drove the car onto the train and sat idly in the driver's seat as Barney and I were carried past the place where the train had let us off a week ago to hike to Portage Glacier. Drove the car off the train at Portage siding and returned it to Harry. Tomorrow Barney and I are booked on the flight from Anchorage to Montana.

June 3 — "I make a silent promise to the birds, whose every action mirrors their determination to succeed in the difficult task that lies before them, that I will not leave this sad and lovely place before they do."

June 1

June 13 —
"All, including Man, struggle to
meet one deadline after another before
the ice fastens its chains around
Melancholy Bay for the winter."

June 13 — Eskimo kids

June 13 — King salmon on drying rack

*June 14 —
Barney watching
salmon hit the net*

June 14 — "Caught some truly grand kings tonight, some better than forty pounds."

June 21 — Loading salmon onto a DC-3

June 22 — Camping on the Melancholy River

July 6 — Drying wet clothes and sleeping bags in rare sunshine

August 4 — Dolly Varden trout

August 7 — "I feel as one who looks through a window in time upon a fantasy of prehistory."

August 7 — "... dozens surge forward into the sea."

August 7 — "The beach is shrouded with a cloud of steam that rises from the huge bodies."

August 7

August 8 — "I decide that my Melancholy hills suggest dinosaurs."
Beluga Rock suggests the head of a rearing tyrannosaurus rex.

August 12

August 16

108

August 14 — Silver salmon

August 19 — Tied-up behind a tender, waiting to sell

110

August 20 — "I sit outside the tent and watch the marsh hawks ride the thermals that rise along my hillside."

August 27 — "Wonderful fishing lately."

Hay rake — Saskatchewan

Autumn

Montana • Saskatchewan • Washington
Arizona • Texas • Mississippi

October 7—The fly rod in my hand is the same...

The fly rod in my hand is the same but everything else is different in Montana. I have spent the summer in a place dominated by water, where dry, firm land by virtue of its scarcity is a thing to be wondered at. Here, the prairie is like the ocean, and this bewitching little brook, bordered by willows, is a meandering green zone of life running through so much parched emptiness. To let the willows close behind me and step into Centenniel Creek is to enter another world. The tight curves and bends are the territory of the mink, the warbler, the whitetail doe. I wade downstream, borne along by the shadowy, moving water. I step into an opening in the willows, into yet another river, one of sunlight. My brain separates the confusion of sensations, the cool water through my waders, the sunlight on my face. Barney plods along at my side, nearly up to his chest, intently watching the fly line as I dribble the worm through the promising holes. Barney's enthusiasm in fishing for these small brook trout kindles mine.

I am delighted to see a dipper, or water ouzel, a nervous, wren-like bird, also working this section of the creek. The small, tail bobbing bird is equally at home flitting like a moving shadow through the air or walking underwater among the pebbles and stones of the stream bottom. To me she seems not so much bird, as nexus between bird and brook trout, just as the wren seems to me to be the nexus between bird and mouse. The dipper is the talisman of tumbling waters, the keeper of our western rivers. When I lived year round in Montana, and Barney and I would fish, in January, the sections of the Big Hole River that were not sheathed in ice, for whitefish, using grubs on the fly rod, we would see the dipper, watching the river through the dead months, until green willow, swallow and cricket, return.

On this day I am surprised to see the little gray perpetual motion machine sitting, as still as a dove, on a stone in the middle of the creek, perhaps in communication with the river muse, or perhaps struck dumb by that tinkling engine of beatitude, Centenniel Creek. It reminds me of the time that a thunderstorm had swept over Barney and me as I cleaned a dozen of the Centenniel's brilliantly colored fall brook trout. I had become aware that, over the sound of the wind and the rattling willows, I could hear the faint piping of a nearby bird, not the song sparrow or the warbler, but an entirely unfamiliar song. It was the dipper, the bird that seems to have personally taken to heart the advice of the most venerable of all fishermen, Izaak Walton, when he said in 1653, "Study to be quiet." She sat not twenty feet away, uncharacteristically moved to song by something in the storm that spoke to her reclusive nature.

October 10 - On this day my father, who has flown out...

On this day my father, who has flown out from North Carolina, is with Barney and me for a week's fishing in Yellowstone Park and today we fish the Firehole River with the sound and smell of exploding geysers, bubbling, boiling mud and hissing fumeroles, constantly in the air. Elk, bison, and man all wade this river in the quicksilver perfection of an Indian summer afternoon. Summer, feeling her death, vibrates at a fine, high pitch. The nocturnal mink is abroad in day. Each wild head is up and listening; change is in the air.

The years that have separated Dad and me fall away like the aspen leaves that spin to the ground. The river sweeps us back to the days we spent together on North Carolina and Virginia's mountain streams, where I was introduced to the rivers, birds and moments which would be the standards by which all other rivers, birds, and moments since, have been measured.

"I have written in this book nearly always of rivers, occasionally of lakes or the salt water, but nearly always of rivers and river fishing. A river is water in its loveliest form; rivers have life and sound and movement and infinity of variation; rivers are veins of the earth through which the life blood returns to the heart. Rivers can attain overwhelming grandeur, as the Columbia does in the reaches all the way from Pasco to the sea; they may slide softly through flat meadows or batter their way down mountain slopes and through narrow canyons; they may be heavy, almost dark, with history, as the Thames is from its mouth at least up to Richmond; or they may be sparkling fresh on mountain slopes through forest and alpine meadows.

"Lakes and the sea have great secret depths quite hidden from man and often almost barren of life. A river too may have its deep and secret places, may be so large that one can never know it properly; but most rivers that give sport to fly-fishermen are comparatively small and one feels that it is within the range of the mind to know them intimately, intimately as to their changes through the seasons, as to the shifts and quirks of current, the sharp runs, the slow glides, the eddies and bars and crossing places, the very rocks of the bottom. And in knowing a river intimately is a very large part of the joy of fly-fishing.

"One may love a river as soon as one sets eyes upon it; it may have certain features that fit instantly with one's conception of beauty, or it may recall the qualities of some other river, well known and deeply loved. One may feel in the same way an instant affinity for a man or a woman and know that here is pleasure and warmth and the foundation of deep friendship. In either case the full riches of the discovery are not immediately released; they cannot be; only knowledge and close experience can release them. Rivers, I suppose, are not at all like human beings, but it is still possible to make apt comparisons; and this is one: Understanding, whether instinctive and immediate or developing naturally through time or grown by conscious effort, is a necessary preliminary to love. Understanding of another human being can never be complete, but as it grows towards completeness, it becomes love almost inevitably. One cannot know intimately all the ways and movements of a river without growing into love of it. And there is no exhaustion to the growth of love through knowledge, whether the love be for a person or a river, because the knowledge can never be complete. One can come to feel in time that the whole is within one's compass, not yet wholly and intimately known, but there for the knowing, within the last little move of reaching; but there will always be something ahead, something more to know."[1]

[1]Roderick L. Haig-Brown, *A River Never Sleeps*, New York, Nick Lyon's Books, 1980.

October 12 – On this day drove just outside the Park...

On this day drove just outside the Park to fish a gem of a high mountain lake, full of small cutthroat trout. Dad, the master of the light line, uses a two pound test line and small wobbling brass spoons and spinners, while I use a six pound test. He catches his limit, and then catches mine too, apologizing all the while.

I listen as Dad talks to another venerable fisherman who sits in a wheelchair, the front wheels several inches into the blue water of this small lake surrounded by rock and sage, with a stringer of native cutthroats snapped to the spokes, as happy and wealthy as any two men on earth. As I watch Dad, with Barney at his side, I feel that the fisherman must surely be a living, breathing metaphor as he casts for a lost innocence, gazing at the mirrored surface as if at a closed window to the pleasures and simplicity of youth.

Driving back into the park to the Inn, the sun's sinking is the pulling of the curtains on nature's perfect performance. As I feed Barney, who must sleep in the camper alone, the flute-like bugling of elk, sounding strangely like the recordings I have heard of whales, is a call to arms among the bulls that slip through the forest and around the edges of the open parklands.

October 16 – After dreaming all summer of the short grass prairie...

After dreaming all summer of the short grass prairie where the sun strikes the hillsides and sets the crickets singing, I am standing there now. I am accustomed to the Alaskan coastal storm systems sliding overhead, their colossal pinwheeling gyres taking on the average, three days to spin down the coastline toward the Aleutian Peninsula. Here it is usually not the storm systems, revolving counterclockwise in this hemisphere, that determine the weather; it is the wind that is the architect of change and while on the ocean, the wind determines the character of the sea, here the undulating surface of the terrain determines the character of the wind where I stand. After walking all morning Barney and I rest in the calm of a windshadow behind a knoll while ten feet away the wind pours through a notch like a cataract. Coming over a crest where it boils over the rounded surface like an airfoil, it is a chilling blast in the face. This time of the year, a north wind drops the temperature and often blows the skies clear, and pushes the big flocks of mallards down from northern Saskatchewan. The most dramatic wind is the Chinook, blowing dry and sad out of the southwest, sometimes raising the temperature nearly 100 degrees in twenty-four hours, turning the landscape, frozen in subzero cold, into one that tinkles miraculously with running water, in a matter of hours.

120

After spending the summer on the spongy tundra, north-central Montana seems to be the most elegant place on Earth for walking. The clean, unencumbered skyline, the line of flight of the sharptailed grouse, make this country seem rarified, like Isak Dinesen's Africa at 6,000 feet. Small boulders lie in the yellowed grass like great Easter eggs. In my long, rambling walks, I see lapland longspurs; could these be some of the birds of my hillside? The sandhill cranes, heard high overhead, occasionally form a lazily rotating vortex, revolving higher and higher until going out of sight between the curving back of the earth and the sun. The jackrabbits have turned white before the snow has come and they startle me as they catapult into the open from practically under my feet. They run with one leg strangely out of stride with the rest, stopping to stand on their hind legs for a better look at Barney, who gives them a short chase. Barney flushes a single sharptail grouse from a copse of Russian olive trees and I kill it, finding the bird's crop full of grasshoppers. We spend the rest of the day working the south facing slopes, for that is where the red winged hoppers rattle drily into flight from underfoot. I cannot get ahead of the one and a half hour law, which states that in a normal season, for each bird put into the backpack, there will be a minimum of one and a half hour's walking. This suits me, for the daily limit of four birds keeps me occupied in my peregrinations for most of the day.

Just before sundown, I drive my Volkswagen bus to a knoll, particular in no way, only one of 10,000 knolls from which the prairie, in the failing light, takes on the visage of enchantment; going from gilded to leaden in half an hour, as the stars begin to appear. At this point I find it difficult to sleep soundly in a house full of the ticking of clocks, the sound of refrigerators and heaters turning on and off, but in particular, full of dead air. I long for the flap of my canvas walls in the wind. I sleep well enough in my bus, which rocks slightly in the gusts. Barney and I are a little like the people of the Sahara, driven into the cities of Algeria by drought, who put their belongings in houses, but sleep in tents in courtyards.

On this night, gazed at Vega, blinking blue and white like a tiny, flashing crystal, now over short grass prairie instead of tundra. While I sit at the table in the bus, reading over the notes I made today, Barney sleeps in the front seat, paws twitching in a dream of birds or fish, or a fight with Jughead. He is too old to protest when I place my wool sweater over his resting form, still bleached auburn by the Alaskan sun. He cannot jump into the front seat after a day's walking; I have to lift him in now. Having "discovered" Montana and Alaska together, we have a bond that only shared hardships and dangers can create. Looking at him, my thoughts fly across eleven years, to the pup that had his first retrieving lessons on brook trout caught on worms in the creek behind the bunkhouse where I was a ranch hand in southwest Montana. His life is drawing to a close, even as the most treasured chapter of mine does likewise.

October 23 – When I was 18, I hitchhiked from North Carolina...

When I was 18, I hitchhiked from North Carolina to Wyoming, worked stacking hay for part of the summer, then backpacked for a week in the Bridger Wilderness. I have never been the same person since that summer and if I could pick one sight, sound or smell that brings back those numbered days of youthful discovery, it would be the smell of sage. When I had come home that summer two decades ago, from time to time I would unscrew the lid on a jar of sage brush I had brought home, and lose myself in a reverie of the land where the Rockies form a misty blue line on the horizon where the prairie stops and the mountains begin in the shimmering silver distance. And on this day I am once again in sage brush country, now as familiar to me as North Carolina's sensuous woodlands once were, and yet the smell of sage still triggers the sinking stomach sensation of wonder, faithfully recorded twenty years ago on such a flawless day as today.

Today's quest is for North America's most dignified and endangered upland game bird, the sage grouse. No other western game bird is so startlingly huge when flushed nor so quiet to wing, considering its great size. The birds have moved from the hay meadows into sage for the winter. Their numbers are good this year, due to the timing of their courtship and nesting, for last year's murderous spring snow storm did not catch the incubating birds on the nest, as it did most other species.

Each year thousands of acres of sage brush are sprayed, chained and plowed under and today, as Barney and I hunt this rolling country, we are seldom out of sight of the encroaching strips of wheat and blocks of pasture land which threaten the critical sage brush habitat of this splendid bird. It is to this spot, when I taught school one hundred miles west of here, that I would come each spring to watch the males display and court on the leks or strutting grounds. In many cases, the leks have been turned into highways or housing developments and these avian dinosaurs, unable to change, nevertheless return to the same location, just as the salmon does, in a uniquely poignant statement of the cruelty of mindless development. I read of one instance where a house was built on top of a sharptail grouse lek. The birds which had traditionally used it returned the following spring to strut on the roof of the structure.

Once located, these birds are not difficult to kill and Barney and I quickly take our limit of three birds. We seldom take more than one limit each season for they are not challenging to shoot and they often taste of sage, especially late in the season, but coming here is part of our autumn trip in years when there is a good population of birds.

One of the nicest things about this part of our fall trip is camping here where the northern lights frequently display this time of year. Shortly after I have cooked supper of fried sage grouse breast and potatoes, I see the lights are going to perform. They begin by forming a poisonous green and silver corona, like a nocturnal rainbow, which separates into two broad, wispy veils which suggest the pipes of a vast, heavenly baroque organ. At midnight, rippling flares begin to walk across the veils, like major and minor chords struck in light rather than sound. The Big Dipper is high in the north sky and will still hold water even at this late hour, but by 5:00 a.m. it will be standing on its handle. Barney and I take a long walk down the gravel road where I am camping for the night. The reading light in the bus is soon a tiny pinpoint of light in the study of still life, of pale, fragrant sage.

October 25 — On this day drove north on the highway...

On this day drove north on the highway that will claim more up-land game birds during the passing of any one week of the year in the state of Montana, than will fall to my gun during Barney's life-time, not to mention its toll of song birds, small mammals, and deer. In the Saskatchewan grain country, where the snow fences and stone piles in the corners of fields give the land a human, hand-worn quality like the terraced hills of Ireland, I stop to watch a great flock of ducks, looking like a cloud of black smoke as they descend on a field of wind-rowed wheat. The mallards number in the thousands as they feed their way down the rows, and those at the rear, realizing that there is little grain left, leapfrog to the head of the line, putting those at the head in the rear, who in turn take to the air briefly to regain their forward position. In this way the flock snakes its way across the endless yellow fields, so like the movement of a toy we used to call a "slinky" that it is quite comical, unless one happens to be a grain farmer.

Barney and I stop at the abandoned homesteads, for they often are the home of a covey of Hungarian partridges. As we hunt the backyard, taken over by wheat grass and full of rusting machinery, I imagine a young couple standing arm in arm with dreams of turning a tiny bit of this endless space into a working farm and passing it on to their children. Where they might have stood in the doorway, a rusty screen door now hangs by one hinge.

From its spider's lair in a grove of olive trees Barney flushes out the friendless great horned owl, which has inherited the home place. In the corner of the yard, the white bones of a cow lie like the scattered pieces of a puzzle. Behind this homestead there is a stockpond now filling with sediment and Barney and I check it to see if it holds mallards. As we sneak up behind the earthen dam, I hiss at Barney to keep him at my side until we are in the dam's shadow. He bounds over the top and the air is full of "northerns," their green heads iridescent in the sun, the sound of straining pinions filling my ears.

November 3 — Spent part of today hunting...

Spent part of today hunting the boggy, bowl-shaped prairie depressions that collect rain water and cool air and hold common snipe as they linger before the coming freeze. Barney, though he does not fancy the odor of the dimunitive relative of the woodcock any more than he does the smell of the woodcock itself, knows his job is to hunt whatever type of cover and game bird is at hand. There is something fascinating about the "eclectic bag." At the end of a day, to take several species of game bird from the backpack, to study the plummage, configuration, and gestalt of the different birds that are the definitive abstractions of each type of habitat and terrain covered that day, is to have before you the multiformity of the day as a whole in tangible form. While hunting is difficult or impossible to justify on a philosophical level, studies by A. Starker Leopold, Gallizioli and others have shown that moderate hunting pressure has little effect on game bird populations. During the 1950's and 60's in America, before the camping and canoeing movements, it was quietly known that the only friends a fishery had were its fishermen. They fought the pollution of their lakes and estuaries and the damming of their rivers largely by themselves. Now, although it is supremely ironic, the most dedicated defenders of game birds are those who hunt them, for no other group watches as closely the destruction of habitat or generates the millions of dollars yearly to restore and protect it. The school girl who feels the urge not merely to look, but to pick and take home a wildflower or any such totem that embodies the wildness and loveliness of a place she has found, has more in common with Barney and me than she might suspect.

Those individuals, who themselves should be vegetarian, who feel it is uncivilized to shoot game birds to eat should view this act as something that is more a part of us than perhaps we would like to admit. The history of Homo sapien stretches back for one half million years, not including the three million years his hominid ancestors roamed the earth. He began to live in villages and cultivate grains and animals only 9,000 years ago in the Middle East. This means that during the history of Man, he has been exclusively a nomadic hunter-gatherer for approximately 98% of his history.

Given the state of the world and the stressful lives many of us face daily, one might well envy the life of a hunter-gatherer, which was much like the life of a baboon today. The baboon begins each day foraging for food for several hours as the "eyelids of the dawn" open. Then the baboon group uses the time when the sun is high to groom and interact with each other within a social framework where both genders have equal status, where each member has an extended family, and the entire group is enveloped in an aura of cooperative energy. In the evening the baboons forage once again for several hours as the sun sinks beneath the plains of Africa, where we too came to be.

Compared to the earth's 4.5 billion year history, 9,000 years is a very short track record indeed, hardly the blink of an eye. He who shoots three sharp-tailed grouse in an afternoon for food, is a time tested part of the landscape. He who clears away wildlife habitat and destroys natural beauty for profit, is not.

Having skirted the snipe bogs, we turn our attention to the business of the day, seeking pheasants. Pheasants are certainly not my favorite bird to hunt; they haunt the cruelest thickets, rather than the open prairie favored by the sharptail grouse. Yet Barney and I spend more time seeking them than any other species, because these adaptable birds are increasing their range as the native game birds dwindle due to habitat destruction, because they are delicious and beautiful, but mostly because the pheasant is

Barney's tour de force; no other bird gets his blood "up" like the rooster that refuses to take to wing. The olfactory duels that are played out in the wild rose thickets that no breed but a springer would even enter, become extremely personalized. This game matches the pheasant's running speed and his considerable cunning against the nose and determination of Barney. On those days when I am able to kill the daily limit of three roosters and Barney flushes yet another one as we walk back to the bus, there are not words to describe the damning look of anathema he gives me when the gun does not speak.

Barney is not the only individual I know who has strong feelings about this handsome import from the Orient. When I taught school in Montana, one of the main considerations in deciding which locations to apply to, was the quality of the game bird habitat in the area. I suppose it was only a matter of natural selection that at one such school I should come to know Ralph Rogers, a falconer and also a biology teacher who had found his way to Wynona for the same reason I had. The bird that had brought him up from Texas was also my favorite game bird, the sharptail grouse, considered by the devout falconer as the "chosen" bird for hawking on this continent. These powerful fliers are the only upland bird, beside the other red-meated upland birds, the ptarmigan and the sage grouse, that can fly from horizon to horizon. The sharptail has impeccable credentials from the fal-coner's point of view. He holds well for the pointing dog, giving time for the falcon to be put aloft, and when flushed, relies on his consummate skill and honesty as a flier as the falcon stoops or dives, making possible an aerial duel that is the heart of Ralph's sport. The falcon, which Ralph diets, showers with a sprinkler, and croons to with an intimacy that makes his good natured wife shake her head, can only make two or three flights per outing. Two kills a week is cause for celebration in this most aesthetic but least pro-ductive method of hunting upland birds. In most instances the grouse outflies the hawk. Listening closely, I have been able to catch phrases like "tactical error" and "faked you out" from Ralph's mutterings as he places the hood over the head of the upset but unrepentant bird. After a particularly humiliating flight, when the sharptail leaves the falcon clutching at empty air with a clever roll-out maneuver, I have seen Ralph's blue blooded Peregrine sitting disconsolate atop a telephone pole or on a high and lonely snag, back turned to the world, refusing to come to hand in spite of Ralph's fervent pleas, bribes, and tantalizingly presented lures. "She's going to make me spend the night sitting under the tree with the spotlight to keep away the great horned owls, again," he had turned and said to me one day as the sun went down, an exquisitely pained expression on his face. It is a tempestuous love affair, this, and I can tell you that with one who calls himself a falconer, as Juliet would learn when she asked, "What's in a name?" … there is more than meets the eye.

At the other end of Ralph's scale of good and evil is the pheasant, which he considers an unpatriotic import, which displaces the innocent, less aggressive native sharptails. The pheasant refuses to flush for the hawk, but chooses to hide ignobly under a creek bank or to squat in an impenetrable briar thicket. When Ralph is able to flush one, as soon as the pheasant sees the hawk diving toward him at approximately two hundred miles per hour, he immediately does the sensible, but in Ralph's eyes, unforgivable, thing, which is to instantly land, hitting the ground running, leaving the hawk in a frustrated state of limbo. Worst of all, and this is a touchy subject between Ralph and me, pheasants attract "gun hunters," who inadvertently shoot some of Ralph's "hawking birds," the sharptails, which frequently precipitates his "death in the family" soliloquy.

The last time I was through Wynona and went with Ralph to watch the hawk at work, the dog had quickly located a small covey of sharptail grouse and pointed them expertly at the far end of a huge field of grain stubble. The hawk had gone up boldly and hovered high above the dog frozen on point, waiting for the flushing of the grouse. But then, instead of waiting for Ralph to walk commandingly in to make the flush and witness closehand "the moment" for which the falconer lives, in a smooth clockwork of motion, the dog had rushed in and flushed the grouse; the hawk stooped nobly, nailing a bird. Unfortunately all this was visible only through binoculars. Ralph turned his grief-stricken face to me, "They won't let me play anymore." Quickly getting a grip on himself, Ralph had gone on to say in his solemn educator's voice, "I am tempted to call this learning, but then I've always said that too much knowledge is a dangerous thing. No one ever said it would be easy."

As Barney and I walk the blackberry thickets and the groves of
conifers along a small stream in Montana's Lewis and Clark
National Forest hoping to flush a ruffed grouse, I watch a Townsend's soletaire defend his winter's food supply, a juniper tree full of
waxy blue berries, against a flock of bohemian waxwings, down
from Canada. As I watch him repeatedly drive off the intruders, I
feel I am watching a western version of an event I witnessed two
thousand miles east of here, nearly a year ago. I had watched, in
North Carolina, a mockingbird, so like the Townsend's soletaire in
personality and appearance, drive a flock of cedar waxwings from
his winter's food supply, a dogwood tree full of red berries. The
scenes, the actors, and the action had been so similar that it seems
impossible that they could have been separated by the Great Plains
and the Appalachians. The birds a continent apart, as well as the
people a culture apart, make me feel as though, while the forms
and faces of the actors may change, the play must be performed
according to the original script, fret as we may.

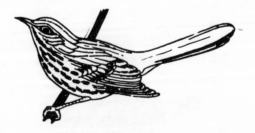

November 15 — Montana's Indian summer and fall colors...

Montana's Indian summer and fall colors have glowed these fleeting weeks and now winter has roughly shouldered them aside. On one side of the Continental Divide my breath smokes in the cold, but two hours' drive west take Barney and me into Washington state's bountiful orchard country, where the wild rosehips are as large as grapes and the cottonwoods still carry their leaves. Returning each fall, the places that remain have become rich in memories. Along the creek I hunted today Barney refused to come to heel three years ago, but kept worrying about a blackberry thicket until a pair of cock pheasants burst from cover; one bird killed cleanly with the right barrel, the other one missed equally cleanly with the left. Just beyond the creek, in a random and seldom visited wood, I could always count on several coveys of California quail. On this day, I see that random wood is no more; having been cleared for pasture. Along a dilapidated fence row, lost in blackberry and other protective winter cover and nesting habitat, Barney and I were once shadowed by a yearling goshawk that flew on each pheasant we flushed, preventing me from shooting lest I hit him, clumsily trying to stay with the birds Barney had put into the air. Today I notice that along that same overgrown fence row there is a series of orange survey flags, telling me that heavy machinery will soon be here to clear this land.

Barney and I will not return to this place next fall, for although the new owner gave us permission to hunt, it is obvious that the farm has fallen into hands eager to put the slumbering creek bottoms and thickets into production. In a few years these hills that have echoed with the crowing of pheasant and the whistle of California quail each spring will be silent, but it is doubtful that the new owner will notice the difference.

November 16 – After the disappointment of yesterday ...

After the disappointment of yesterday I have driven south to the Snake River Breaks, near Clarkston, Washington, where no tractor will ever drill wheat seed or clear away wild game habitat, for there are only the folded and convoluted hills of basaltic rock, wild grasses and the chukar, the hardy partridge introduced from India. Barney and I quest along the flows of lava rock now covered with light green lichens and blue bunch wheatgrass. The derisive calls of these handsome, red-legged game birds echo off the rock walls as they watch my painfully slow progress upward. The weather here is dry and gentle, yet it feels almost coastal. In these near vertical grasslands, over 100 species of song birds have been recorded, as well as elk, bighorn sheep, black bear and an occasional cougar. The wild grass, which is nearly as lush as when Chief Joseph and his band of Nez Perce wintered here, has erased nearly all traces of the homestead days when the mail boat that threaded Hells Canyon brought the only news of the outside world. However, the fate of the great rivers of the Pacific Northwest is sealed forever. Looking down the Snake toward the point where it meets the Columbia, it is sad to contemplate that the Columbia, once the pride of the Northwest, is now a series of long lakes. Her salmon runs had no equal in North America, including Alaska's river systems. They are now a thing of the past, first choked off by fish wheels and unrestricted gill netting, then locked out forever by concrete dams. In the ultimate statement of man's hubris and disrespect for both the natural world and his own offspring, he shackled and impounded this grand river in a series of eleven dams, stilling all but 50 miles of the once free-flowing giant. How prophetic were the words of Chief Seattle in 1854, when he called the coming of the white man "The end of living and the beginning of survival."

The Snake River is damned too, by twelve impoundments built by the Idaho Power Company and the Corps of Engineers. The final straw, the Asotin Dam, would have stilled the last free-flowing stretch, Hells Canyon, and flooded one of America's national treasurers. However, in unanimity, ranchers, sportsmen, naturalists, people from all walks of life, came together at the hearings for the proposed final dam and said, "Enough!"

When the Europeans discovered America they attacked the forests with a religious fervor, vanquishing the natural world and the original inhabitants, over whom they felt God had given them "dominion." Unhappily, that prideful attitude remains, but here, overlooking the Snake, who still flings her icy waters down this mile-deep gorge in mountainous waves and humbling rapids, there is a feeling of hope. Perhaps the white man has finally begun to put himself in perspective.

In time it may be proven that only with a harmonious relationship with Nature can Man keep his wits. One look at a newspaper tells the reader that something is terribly wrong. Surely, as an insurance, we should protect more than the two percent of America presently set aside and, perhaps more important, restore the natural beauty within our cities and in all the places where people live out their daily lives. Few have the opportunity to backpack in Alaska; the preservation concept can be applied along the highway right-of-way as well as in the Brooks Range. It may be that in preserving our wilderness and making natural beauty accessible, we are preserving ourselves. It would appear that without access, on a daily basis, to subtle natural clues that define us, we are no better than any other animal placed in a stressful, unnatural environment. No creature thus confined is allowed his dignity. It may be that the old verities of altruism, compassion and the loving of others rather than oneself, are not really virtues at all, but are merely survival tools that make socialized living possible and have evolved wherever Man has been tutored by Nature, draconian teacher though She is.

November 17— This day finds me driving south,

This day finds me driving south, headed for the Grand Canyon. Hour after hour my vintage Volkswagen camper, "The White Elephant," rolls along at its top speed of 50 miles per hour, as Barney sleeps in the passenger seat.

We stop for a break in the driving near Boise, Idaho, and go for a walk, and Barney quickly picks up several dozen cockelburrs in his ears. I pull them out, one at a time as I have done a thousand times before, imploring him to stay out of the "burrs." Barney's thoughtful yellow eyes seem to pose the question, "How can these fiendish seed pods bear the same name as the sweetly scented 'birds' we quest after each fall?" Yet this and other hopelessly inexplicable things are accepted on blind faith. In years past, when I have cut off my beard, such a transformation does not earn a second glance from Barney, who knows me whether fair or foul.

Some years ago Barney was confounded but not fooled by a diabolical experiment whose authorship I must claim with embarrassment. I had taped my voice calling Barney, which I played at one end of a room while I sat silently at the other. Barney had walked to the strange black box from which his master's voice called, sniffed it, sighed deeply, and then walked slowly to me and put his head in my lap, gazing with long-suffering forebearance at my evil face.

137

November 20 - As I drive South the colors shift...

As I drive south the colors shift from the stark and contrasting
stands of coniferous timber and white crowned mountains, into a
light dun in Utah, but in Arizona the countryside spreads a peacock's fan of soft tans, pinks, and pale ochre. As I take Barney for
yet another walk, I kneel down to examine ant mounds of sand like
multi-colored bits of glass. The Spanish bayonet, the greasewood
and cactus seem to stand in a stillness of death, a world removed
from Centenniel Creek's tinkling, life giving waters. But we drive
on late into the night, and it is then that the desert comes to life.
The ruby eyes of fox and hare float through the outer range of my
headlights. The wind and the moonlight, loving the openness of
this place, transform the sculpted rocks into an exhibit of silvered
forms and shapes, a well-spring of aphrodisiac scents. In the morning, under the sage brush, the fine grained sand is a tablet that has
recorded the wanderings of beetle, rattlesnake and lizard. After our
walk through the dunes, our footprints have deeply scarred the
pink and orange sands, but a windstorm will erase the record of my
brief passage, just as easily as the beetle's.

November 21 - There are two Grand Canyons.

There are two Grand Canyons, the Canyon of light, the very heart of Earth, broached to wind and sun, a highway going backward in time for millions of human lifetimes, composed of the bones of ancient pilgrims, a series of ever simpler Canterbury Tales winding down and down until finally the last tale becomes only a riddle, posed by the river; Why?

And there is the Canyon of darkness, the one that waits for the orange sunball to rise over the blackened rim, the one that emerges when the leading edge of a storm front glides overhead like a heavenly manta ray, draining away the Canyon's color, turning the Canyon of light into a great wound, where wind and water have cut to the very bone and sinew of Earth, down to the time when the wind was like a knife from beyond the stars, before the dawn of consciousness, before yearning one for another. This is the great, dark gorge that I imagine Man creeping into, thousands of years before Christ, borne along by his courage, his voice softly echoing off the rocky walls in utterances we would recognize today. It fills me with a fierce pride.

November 23 - On this day Barney and I fish the Colorado River...

On this day Barney and I fish the Colorado River below Glen Canyon Dam for the rainbow trout that have been introduced there. We are only the latest of many to visit these canyonlands. The split willow twig figures, some of which were found still standing in the dust of caves in the canyon, suggest that man was familiar with this place 4,000 years before John Wesley Powell floated his expedition through it in 1869. The Anasazi, thought to be the direct ancestors of the present day Hopi Indians of northern Arizona, probably arrived here around the time of Christ. They lived throughout the Canyon, on the rims in the summer where they farmed, and in the lower elevations in winter, where temperatures remained warmer.

The ruins of the ancient ones are enduring and evocative, still in harmony with the setting. The evidence of the hand of modern man is not. By the end of the 19th century the burro had become well established in the canyon, and began to reduce the food and water available to the indiginous big game species, the big horned sheep and deer. Their overgrazing has created serious erosion problems. The Glen Canyon Dam has dramatically altered the character of the Colorado River. Since the annual floods have been halted by the dam, rock falls and bank slumping are no longer swept away each spring. Many of the rapids are rising in height and severity. However, the cold, silt-free waters that are released from 200 feet below the surface of Lake Mead and flow through the dam, are ideal for the rainbow trout that Barney and I seek today.

The light wind swirls about the limestone faces composed of the organic remains of coral and shell, carrying scents that speak of the junipers and ponderosa pine of the Kaibab plateau, and of the pinons of the mesas of the ancient Hopis. I suppose one could compare many geological features to Michaelangelo's "captive" sculptures, which are unfinished and still wait for the imprisoning marble to be chipped away to reveal the final perfection of form. However, these canyonlands of the Colorado River have been pared down to their very pastel essence from the rocky matrix. They stand as monuments to the oneness of life and death, yesterday and today.

Since time has left much of the Southwest with no topsoil, it need not fear the plow. Much of it stands unfettered and ethereal.

"In New Mexico he always awoke a young man; not until he rose and began to shave did he realize that he was growing older. His first consciousness was a sense of the light, dry wind blowing in through the windows, with the fragrance of hot sun and sage-brush and sweet clover; a wind that made one's body feel light and one's heart cry "Today, today," like a child's.

"...He had noticed that this peculiar quality in the air of new countries vanished after they were tamed by man and made to bear harvests ... one could breathe that only on the bright edges of the world, on the great grass plains or the sage brush desert.

"...Something soft and wild and free, something that whispered to the ear on the pillow, lightened the heart, softly, softly picked the lock, slid the bolts and released the spirit of man into the wind, into the blue and gold, into the morning, into the morning."[1]

[1]Willa Cather, *Death Comes for the Archbishop,* New York, Alfred A. Knopf, 1970.

December 3 — On this day as we stopped in Muenster,

On this day as we stopped in Muenster, Texas, Barney chased the first squirrel we have seen since leaving North Carolina last spring, up a tree. I still remember the look of consternation on his face when he, a dog of the prairies, born in Great Falls, Montana, had seen his first tree climbing "rabbit." It is almost precisely here that the country ceased being western and began to feel distinctly "southern," the air heavy with nostalgia, the English looking oaks dark against the evening sky.

December 5 - On this day Barney and I are near Natchez,

On this day Barney and I are near Natchez, Mississippi. From the swampy river bottoms come the shrill whistle of cedar waxwings, the hooting of owls and the tapping of many woodpeckers. It seems strange, after seeing the red-shafted flicker all fall, to now see his yellow-shafted eastern cousin. Stranger yet, in Barney's eyes, if his cocked ears and raised right forepaw are any indication, are the fox squirrels with their startling orange tails. In the grass, thousands of spider webs glisten in the morning sun.

I would like to stop and hunt woodcock in this area, for this is where most of the North American birds winter, but I only shoot the game birds I can eat, and it is well known that these fascinating and endearing birds, in addition to having their habitat destroyed, carry high levels of heptachlor epoxide and a host of other toxins. According to a recently completed Ford study, the U.S. leads the developed nations in birth defects and one of the three major causes is environmental toxins. All of our game birds, from the endrin carrying ducks of the Pacific Northwest to the contaminated woodcock of the Mississippi-Louisiana lowlands, are a dependable and pathetic barometer of this.

*August 16 — Rainbow trout
caught on sculpin imitation*

*September 23 — "In the yin yang of this place
it seems that one never really gets ahead,
that the caprice of Nature and the limitation
of Man's machinery and wisdom dictate
that this place will ever be true to its name."*

145

September 24 — "From a distance, the glacier looks like a highway, complete with a center line."

146

September 25 — "... a southeast wind has blown large bergs against the shoreline."

August 30 — Snug Cove
(my boat barely visible at anchor)

September 28 — "... opening briefly into
deciduous forest as we drive south."

148

September 27 — Fall colors along the Denali Highway

October 10 —
Yellowstone Park elk

October 7 — "To let the willows close
behind me and step into Centennial Creek
is to step into another world."

150

October 10 —
Firehole River, Yellowstone Park

October 10 — Jager and Don Rice,
fly fishermen consummate

151

October 12 — "As I watch Dad, with Barney at his side, I feel that the fisherman must be a living, breathing metaphor as he casts for a lost innocence."

152

October 16 — "... paws twitching in a dream of birds, or fish, or a fight with Jughead."

October 25 — "From his spider's lair in a grove of olive trees, Barney flushes out the friendless great horned owl who has inherited the home place."

November 3 — Ralph and his falcon

November 15 — Mountain goat kid,
photographed on the Continental Divide at Logan Pass
on Going to the Sun Highway, Glacier Park, Montana

155

November 20 — "... in Arizona the countryside spreads a peacock's fan of soft tans, pinks, and pale ochre."

April 4 — "As Ty and I walk along the tidal basin under the cherry trees toward the Jefferson Memorial, Barney strains against his leash when he recognizes that archetypal form, a man with a fishing rod in his hands."

May 24 — "The dark tracts of timber are broken by balds and parklands."

May 28 — "Today I have returned to Yellowstone Park, which seems to be emerging from a deep and fitful sleep."

June 8 — Cape Flattery — Olympic Peninsula

Cape Hatteras Lighthouse — North Carolina

Winter

North Carolina • South Carolina

December 20 - On this day Dad and I stand looking...

On this day Dad and I stand looking out the window where he has
sprinkled bird feed on the icy patio of the back porch and we watch
Barney methodically lick it up in anteater fashion. His solemn eyes
are fixed upon us as we stand in the window and as much as say,
"Behold a truly sophisticated dog and omnivore." Dad tells me that
he has a resident sharp shinned hawk that occasionally takes a bird
from his feeder and that he regularly sees red tailed hawks sitting in
the hickory tree in the back yard. We decide that this new phe-
nomenon must have resulted from the clean farming techniques
and sub-development of nearby farms and woodlands that have
reached the point where habitat destruction in this part of North
Carolina has become so complete that the eradication of hawk
prey species has forced them to come into town where there is an
abundant supply of song birds. The native quail, woodcock, and
cottontail rabbits have been replaced by species that thrive on
man's by-products and garbage; the starling, the grackle and that
carrion eating contemporary of the dinosaur, the opossum.

   In the nooks and corners of this house are relics and photographs that bring to mind a time when this area was rich in wild
game. It was to this area of North Carolina that men with names
like Morgan, Cress, and Dodge came from New York to the lodges
they leased, to hunt the quail that have since vanished as the
countryside was sterilized. Even when I was a boy, on my bicycle I
could reach ponds and woodlands where I had my first experiences
with nature. They have all disappeared. I think sadly of the youths
of today who will not have the experiences in nature that Dad and
I did. My father grew up in a world rich in sensory experiences,
where the first thing he heard in the morning was the sound of
horse's hooves on cobblestones, as ice and milk were delivered and
the last was of fires being laid for the night in each bedroom. In the

world of his youth, all things were possible. He believed that the hummingbirds that came to my grandmother's flower garden were fairies. His imagination is, to this day, a thing I wonder at. My own is much the lesser in comparison and the youths I knew as students when I taught here seemed to spiral ever downward.

It seems to me, on this day that is flawless, but I have no place to go, that among the people of the East, who have no vast and empty skies, no Grand Canyon, no Rocky Mountains, few wild and lonely beaches, no place of natural wonder left intact where one can go and feel dwarfed by nature and draw from an energy source greater than himself, that there is here a smouldering resentment that has created a great negative energy. If it is true as Einstein said, that imagination is more important than knowledge, then it may be that the plundering of the land that was our heritage, for profit, and the sterile minds that ensue, may be the nemesis of free enterprise.

January 10 – This afternoon Barney and I walk the beaches...

This afternoon Barney and I walk the beaches of Cape Hatteras, on North Carolina's Outer Banks, where the candy cane lighthouse, the tallest in America, stands facing the wintry ocean. Built to warn ships of the treacherous "Graveyard of the Atlantic," an area where the cold arctic current meets the warm Gulfstream, and of Diamond Shoals, it stood approximately 1,000 yards from the ocean in 1870 when it was completed. On this day the surf comes nearly to the foot of the sand buttress at the base.

From stations seven miles apart along this beach, men of the U.S. Life Saving Service used horses to pull heavy wooden lifeboats into the pounding surf and then rowed out to foundered ships to bring the passengers ashore. This beach is protected now and Barney disappears into the thickets of southern bayberry, juniper, yaupon and myrtle to chase marsh rabbits, the dark furred cousin of the cottontail. After the sun sinks from sight and the ocean turns leaden gray, the beam from the lighthouse becomes a glowing shaft which revolves high overhead like the luminary second hand of a huge clock. As the night gathers in strength, Barney and I walk far up the beach until the light is a thin, yellow finger probing into the black vastness over the booming of the waves on the shore. As I walk I think of the Oregon Inlet bridge, which I crossed this morning to come here. It was built across one of the most dynamic and highest energy outlets of the entire east coast, historically migrating southward at the rate of 100 feet per year, making constant dredging a necessity as Man tries to force the channel to remain where he wants it. The inlet, which until recently, has allowed a free exchange of salt water into Albemarle Sound, allowing it to remain a viable brackish water fishery, is now choked off. The complex brackish water ecosystem is rapidly dying; all because Man insists that Oregon Inlet shall remain where he built his bridge to cross it.

"Some 2,500 years ago the citizens of Carthage, a Phoenician people, built a harbor along the shores of the Gulf of Tunis in North Africa. This harbor, from which Hannibal sailed to attack Rome, is still used today by small Arab fishing boats.

"A few hundred years later and some twenty miles away, the Romans, a mightier people, built the seaport of Utica. North Africa was the breadbasket of the Roman Empire, and across the docks of Utica flowed huge quantities of food and treasure to be shipped to the motherland. Today, a tourist standing atop the highest column in the ruins of Utica can no longer see the sea. The shoreline has moved 17 kilometers seaward, away from what was once the harbor.

"The Carthaginians were careful to design to live with nature. The Romans, the first practitioners of brute-force technology, chose to confront, alter, and destroy nature. What the Romans didn't realize was that in the long run, nature always wins at the shoreline."[1]

On a trip home in recent years, I had come to Albemarle Sound with a friend of mine who moved here to live in the area where, in a little publicized but unique natural blessing, eastern North Carolina had been endowed with extraordinarily productive salt, brackish, and fresh water fisheries. He is the only person I know who can identify every bird and nearly every butterfly as

[1]Orrin H. Pilkney, Jr., William J. Neal, Orrin H. Pilkney, Sr., Stanley R. Riggs, *From Currituck to Calabash: Living With North Carolina's Barrier Islands,* Research Triangle Park, North Carolina, North Carolina Science and Technology Research Center, 1980.

well. He had wetted his fingers in the sound and tasted them and had said in digust, "Hardly a taste of salt today." He had gone on to say that with the plugged inlet, the algae blooms caused by overuse of nitrogen based fertilizer and the siltation from topsoil loss, the fisheries were dying. I asked him if he still loved the tidewater country as he had. "It's as if your wife had cancer; you would still love her, but it wouldn't be the same," he replied.

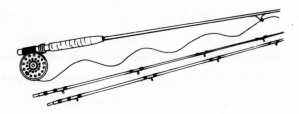

March 2 — Last night pulled the white elephant...

Last night pulled the White Elephant into a palmetto grove in
Edisto Beach State Park, not far from Charleston, South Carolina,
and slept with the sound of the surf only a few yards away. This
morning Barney and I walk through Five Oaks woods where the
live oaks bend their gauzy, vaulted branches over sandy lanes that
are scribed by the neat and sharp-hoofed whitetailed deer each
moonlit night while the wind off the salt marshes moves the fes-
toons of Spanish moss in a calypso of mystery and motion. One
Carolina wren calls and dozens answer from the thick brush where
I imagine diamondback and canebrake rattlesnakes must lie
watching Barney and me on the path, with their lidless, yellow
eyes, until the whole woods echoes momentarily with the harsh
scolding of the wrens. A pileated woodpecker lands nearby on a
rotten snag of a live oak and I watch this crow sized bird, the
Michaelangelo of woodpeckers, as his slow and methodical tap-
tap-tapping becomes the only sound in this bottomland that holds
sounds and smells captive. His strokes are as deliberate and meticu-
lous as a sculptor and after each one, he draws back his head and
inspects his work. Rather than use the air hammer approach of the
lesser woodpeckers, his brilliant, red crowned head, tilting one way
then another, is drawn back in exaggerated, snake like motions
after each stroke as he watches his hole grow in size, until he is satisfied. I then watch him, through my binoculars, as he runs his
long, pointed tongue into the cavity to extract the ants he seeks.
Below his perch on the ground, pieces of the soft, rotten wood
have formed an astonishingly large pile. He flies away, filling the
still woods with his call, nearly identical to the flicker's.

Barney and I continue our walk through these woods which
lack the colors of the desert Southwest, the feeling of vastness of
the Prairie, the grandeur of the Pacific Northwest, but which have
instead a deep and powerful ambience of sensuality. I remember, as
a youth, walking through woods such as these in the summer dusk,

168

still dripping after a sudden rain, heavy with the smell of honey-suckle blossom, lightning bugs blinking softly off and on like desire itself, feeling as potent and disquieted as any character in Tennessee Williams' plays.

In my father's house is a photograph of my great-grandfather, Captain John Fry, holding a wild turkey he had shot in this area of South Carolina. He came here from Greensboro to hunt and fish in the late 1800's in woods as deep and mysterious as the woods of Faulkner's Yoknapatawpha County, Mississippi. Now Five Oaks woods is a tiny oasis in a sprawl of timbered out swampland and weekend retreats, and even more damning, huge "mega-farms." I look out across the vast plowed fields, whose topsoil turns the rivers red after each rain. Because of monoculture agriculture, U.S. farmers lose 1200 pounds of topsoil for each 1800 pounds of grain sold, for a loss of 5 billion tons each year. The land which once comprised a hundred small, family farms is now one sterile giant, where every tree and briar thicket and derelict homestead has been razed and plowed under by diesel four wheel drive tractors whose headlights move inexorably through the night during the planting months.

Many societies have tried the "megafarm" idea, including the Romans, who turned their cultivation over to slaves, and none have survived the ensuing loss of the work ethic and sense of identity.

"Our economy now seems set up to wreck the family and the community, wreck the environment, and at the same time employ people to run around trying to patch it back together. If we changed the game, though, we could employ millions of people by, say, going back to labor-intensive organic farming, building a solar and renewable energy industry, or by deciding to go back to two mail deliveries a day — as we used to have in Britain — or any number of things that would be more socially useful.

169

"...I think there's going to be a long slide of one system, and at the same time a worldwide resurgence of a much older system that's been there all the time — one based on sustainable agriculture and the deep-rooted cultural values we put away during the brief rise of industrialism."[1]

In this area there is lingering superstition, a feeling that those of the spirit world who either choose to remain or somehow must remain, still hover about the places they walked in life. I wonder, if they exist and if they think and feel, what are their thoughts as they watch their sanctuaries obliterated? They must be like the displaced animals that fade pathetically away in quiet starvation, undetected by anyone. I think of the Cape Hatteras Lighthouse and wonder if, like the bell that tolls for thee, the ocean beseiged structure is not a symbol for the nation whose first English colony became "the Lost Colony" not sixty miles from where the yellow beam of the light revolves like the second hand on a clock that may indicate the approach of midnight.

"Man is flying too fast for a world that is round.
Soon he will catch up with himself in a great
rear-end collision and Man will never know
that what hit him from behind was Man."

James Thurber

One hundred miles down the coastline from this place, Man has reached the true nadir in his relationship with his environment at the Savannah Nuclear Waste Repository. Here radioactive waste is drained directly into the delta of the Savannah River, the

[1]Hazel Henderson, "Futurist, the New Age Interview," *New Age Journal*, Brighton, Massachusetts, March 1984

swamp itself having become radioactive, where it will leave a legacy of cancer, death and mutation for millions of years into the future. Instead of learning to conserve, Man continues to build new reactors and create new radioactive waste, and yet there will probably never be a safe way to dispose of it. At the present time there is enough high level radioactive waste to fill the Rose Bowl stadium thirty times.

Nathaniel Hawthorne wrote a short story entitled "Rappaccini's Daughter." It is about an evil doctor named Rappaccini who cares more for science than for mankind to the point that he experiments with human life to add to his knowledge. His grandest experiment involves dangerous tamperings with the fundamentals of nature and results in his own daughter's death.

I knew a "Rappaccini's Daughter" when I came to Montana at the age of 23. I fished and fell in love with a river named the Clark's Fork of the Columbia with all the passion of youth, but in time learned that the entire flood plain of the river was saturated with arsenic and mercury from the mining waste of the Anaconda Company. Each heavy rain washes a "slug" of poisonous metals into the river, killing some of her trout, and all of those that live in the river have an elevated content of dangerous elements. The arsenic and mercury will be there forever, for there is no way to remove it from the sand and from between the stones and pebbles of the river bottom. The Anaconda Company has closed its doors and moved away, leaving no one accountable. The Clark's Fork still flows as beautiful and as cursed as ever, this "Rappaccini's River" that beguiled me, as the dream of cheap inexhaustible power from splitting the atom has beguiled Man. The last sentence of Hawthorne's story is "Rappaccini! Rappaccini! and is this the upshot of your experiment!" Could the upshot of our experiment with free enterprise and democratic rule be an everlasting legacy worse than Rappaccini's?

171

Cherry blossoms — Washington, D.C.

Spring

Washington, D.C. • North Carolina • Virginia
Nebraska • Montana • Olympic Peninsula, Washington
Vancouver Island, British Columbia

April 4 – Barney and I are in the nation's capital on this day...

Barney and I are in the nation's capital on this day of clear skies and cherry blossoms. Today Washington has the feel of a modern Camelot, an emerald city in a nation chosen to test the ideal of freedom as no other ever has nor ever will again. My friend Ty Planz, the assistant manager of one of Montana's waterfowl refuges, is in Washington on business and I have driven up from North Carolina to see him. I associate Ty with a khaki uniform and Montana's boundless sky and rolling prairie, and it seems strange indeed to see him here in a coat and tie, walking among these well-heeled Washingtonians. As Ty and I walk along the tidal basin under the cherry trees toward the Jefferson Memorial, Barney strains against his leash when he recognizes that archetypal form, a man with a fishing rod in his hands. In this civilized setting the provincial Barney chases squirrels up trees and flushes pigeons with a passion that turns the heads and raises the eyebrows of elegant passersby.

In the afternoon I dive south into Virginia to walk the Civil War battlefields. Here the hardwood trees stand in somber and ironic testimony to the natural blessing that has been ruthlessly squandered in perverted consummation of the freedom that was bought so dearly. The words of Lincoln's Gettysburg Address come to mind, "Fourscore and seven years ago our fathers brought forth on this continent a new nation, conceived in liberty and dedicated to the proposition that all men are created equal. Now we are engaged in a great civil war, testing whether that nation, or any nation so conceived and so dedicated, can long endure. We are met on a great battlefield of that war. We have come to dedicate a portion of that field as a final resting place for those who here gave their lives that that nation might live. It is altogether fitting and proper that we should do this. But, in a larger sense, we cannot dedicate — we cannot consecrate — we cannot hallow — this ground. The brave men, living and dead, who struggled here have consecrated it far above our poor power to add or to detract. The world will little note nor long remember what we say here, but it can never forget what they did here. It is for us, the living, rather to be dedicated here to the unfinished work which they who fought here have thus far so nobly advanced. It is rather for us to be dedicated to the great task remaining before us — that from these honored dead we take increased devotion to that cause for which they gave the last full measure of devotion; that we here highly resolve that these dead shall not have died in vain; that this nation, under God, shall have a new birth of freedom; and that government of the people, by the people, for the people, shall not perish from the earth."

When I think of the freedom that Barney and I have taken for granted, of the places and the people between here and Melancholy Bay that we have known, it seems, in looking across this vastness of space and human experience that here will be answered the question of Man's nature, be he essentially base, or essentially noble? Can man live with the responsibility that accompanies freedom as well and eagerly as he fights to gain it? No nation will ever again be blessed with such a natural dowry of timber, topsoil, minerals, fresh water and coastline, nor with a population that is so truly a metaphor for all mankind. Each day the sun rises over the Atlantic, strikes the white stone of the Washington edifice, rolls across the skies of the American heartland, gilds McKinley Park's Mt. Denali, in Alaska, higher than Everest in vertical relief, and finally wakes humble little Melancholy Bay with its huddled covey of plywood shacks, and one cannot but feel that truly all the world's a stage and one cannot but hope that within the heart of hearts of each of us, the actors, enlightenment rather than greed will prevail more often than not.

May 6 — On this day I am walking the deserted grounds...

On this day I am walking the deserted grounds of a summer camp near Brevard, North Carolina, that I attended for several seasons when I was a boy. Each day after supper we had several hours of free time and it was then that I would wade the little bays and coves of the lake that was the heart of the camp, casting about for brook trout, lost in a daydream of the time when these green ridges echoed with gunshots and the drum of horse's hooves as grudges were settled in blood feud fashion, laying the fly on the water as the winnowing call of the whippoorwill bestowed upon the cool, heavy stillness of these mountain hollows, a heart rending sweetness. On this day as Barney and I stand looking across that same lake which now looks very small, old Norm Sloan, the patriarch of the camp, here making preparations for the coming summer, walks slowly across the earthen dam in a gait that I still remember from over two decades ago. I identify myself, one of thousands of boys he has watched come and go, and he surprises me by saying, "I remember you; you're the one who wanted to stay in the mountains and fish." As I drive out the dirt road that I walked so many times as a barefoot boy, now in a Volkswagen bus bearing Alaska license plates, I find myself wondering once again; is one born to do what he will do? Does he really choose his road? I decide that it does not really matter; it is certainly a more interesting trip for not knowing.

From Brevard I drive west toward Tennessee and as I wind through the mountain valleys, there seems to be a lingering sadness from the time when most of these highlands were cut off from the rest of the world in a tragic way that we of the age of television and highways cannot comprehend. Here, until recently, old world dialects were still quite evident. The random mountain homes seem from a bygone age; the following account dates from 1901. "These Kentucky mountaineers are not only cut off from the outside world, but they are separated from each other. Each is confined to his own locality, and finds his little world within a radius of a few miles from his cabin. There are many men in these mountains who have never seen a town, or even the poor village that constitutes their county-seat. ... The women ... are almost as rooted as the trees. We met one woman who, during the twelve years of her married life, had lived only ten miles across the mountain from her own home, but had never in this time been back home to visit her father and mother. Another back in Perry county told me she had never been farther from home than Hazard, the county-seat, which is only six miles distant. Another had never been to the post-office, four miles away; and another had never seen the ford of the Rockcastle River, only two miles from her home, and marked, moreover, by the country store of the district."[1]

The apple tree that stands nearby in the pasture of this small farm may have been a source of deliverance that we of today cannot grasp. On this spring day the mourning doves are flying like kestrels, with exaggerated wing beats and long glides, giving shape and form to the dalliance that rides the light wind like thistledown.

[1]Horace Kephart, *Our Southern Highlanders*, Knoxville, The University of Tennessee Press, 1976.

May 7—I have continued my drive west...

I have continued my drive west and today spent the afternoon hiking the Appalachian Trail at Newfound Gap. As I walk the ridges of these ancient, rounded mountains, the oldest in America, on one of the longest footpaths in the world, I look east into North Carolina and west into Tennessee. The lush hills and valleys are like a vast arboretum whose respiring vegetation creates the haze that gave the Blue Ridge Mountains their name.

In the winter these hills look naked and defeated, but on this day in May, from the endless rolling verdance of the Smokies emanates the power of enchantment. Before me stretches the home of the whippoorwill, the ginseng plant, the banjo player, and the stage for unrequited love, according to the folk songs of the area. Any of the coves and glades that recede out of sight is a botanical garden like no other in the earth's temperate zone. The blossoming locust trees and mountain azaleas shade the strumps of ancient chestnut trees felled years ago by the timbermen who missed not a single drainage or pocket as far as the eye can see.

May 8 - Today I have come to Joyce Kilmer Memorial forest,

Today I have come to Joyce Kilmer Memorial forest, dedicated to the man who wrote the poem, "Trees" before he fell in World War I. Here stands one of the few remaining groves of virgin hardwoods. The size of the giant poplars gives the same feeling of awe as the Douglas firs of the rain forests of the west coast. Some of them have trunks nearly ten feet thick. The footpath that winds through this little memorial forest, centuries in the making, spared because of its inaccessibility, echoes softly with the voices of those who have come to see what was once commonplace.

After my walk, Barney and I sit on the stones of Little Santeetlah Creek and watch the tiger swallowtail and eastern black swallowtail butterflies, as one after another flies dreamily down the corridor above the brook, like blossoms taken to wing.

May 9-Stopped at a grist mill on the Dan River...

Stopped at a grist mill on the Dan River where Dad and I fished for
trout on May weekends such as this one, years ago. Spoke with Mr.
Porter, still grinding corn in the same fashion as his father had
before him. He asks me how my father is, then proceeds to tell me
in an unceasing torrent of striking images, in the tradition of oral
storytelling that was both artful and purposeful, of the tornado
that had touched down here several weeks ago. "I was standing
right here when I heard it. Came across the river, sucked up water
and threw it all over the mill. The timbers groaned and squealed
when the thing passed by; popped out exactly seven panes of glass
out of over a hundred, not one more! Tore that beech tree in half,
and never even blowed off my hat, and me standing not fifty feet
from it." The words of Einstein again flash through my mind, "...our
science, measured against reality, is primitive and childlike ..." but
there is no time for reflecting for Mr. Porter continues. "And there
was the flood of 1979. Covered the generator and drive gears under
three feet of mud. Was all summer muckin' it out. Almost closed
the mill down, but I figure when the mill goes, I'll soon follow."

I drive away with a five pound sack of corn meal in the bus, a
present from Mr. Porter. I find myself wondering how it can be that
this man has apparently not aged in the ten years that have passed
since Dad and I were last here. Perhaps the waters of the Dan that
spill from the mill race and turn the stone wheels are those for
which Ponce de Leon searched.

On this day Barney and I walk through a grove of deciduous trees northeast of Mt. Airy, North Carolina. I am looking for warblers, which are migrating through the southeastern states on their way to nest in the forests of Canada. The leafy canopy overhead echoes with the ringing calls of the tiny wood warblers. Over the rolling Appalachians, sensuality is a softly pounding drum. The warm air is saturated with the perfume of blossom and the pheremone of moth and centipede. The lusty scents wash over these foothills in an irresistible tide of beckoning. The rite of spring is marked by dancers in every cove and glen, underneath every leaf and stone.

The mountain storms seem to draw their strength from a purely mystical source, as compared with the coastal storms spawned by the sea. They strike the mass of this wood like the sails of a great green fleet, filling the hollows with a soft, yet vast and powerful, rustle. Often they are accompanied by thunder, that tympanic id and alter ego of the aurora, which makes Barney huddle against my leg, blinking and cringing with each crashing salvo, right paw raised in protest, the whites of his eyes showing. Hearing my quiet laugh at his histrionics, he suspects he will live to tell of these lightning storms, that, in terms of sheer dramatics, dwarf anything that Alaska or Montana can produce. When the drumming of rain stops, within minutes this misty, dripping greenwood rings once again with birdsong. In the aftermath of the thunderstorm I see that the dogwoods, crouching like shy, fair haired children at the feet of the taller beeches and poplars, have lost many of their white petals, now scattered on the leaves of the forest floor.

May 12 - On this day, as I sit on my father's front porch,

On this day, as I sit on my father's front porch, I am shocked to hear the flute-like song of the Swainson's thrush, which I hear in the thickets that surround my tent each Melancholy summer. For me, the call of this shy thrush somehow sums up Melancholy Bay's wild, clean asceticism like no other sound. As if to underscore the isolation of one who leads a solitary and migratory lifestyle himself, even when he comes "home," I realize with a slight feeling of wonderment, that I may well be the only individual in the city who knows that this flight of small, olive-colored thrushes have paused here as they move across the continent.

There apparently was a time when the people of the eastern states knew well the habits and characteristics of their birds, if the names they gave them are any indication. The song sparrow was known as "everybody's darling," the kingbird was the "bee martin," the redstart was "the firetail," the catbird, that talented mimic, was known as "the slate-colored mockingbird," the indigo bunting, "the blue canary," and the towhee was "the swamp robin."

I watch the children playing in the school yard across the street from my father's house. Most of them have been told that this is the week for city elections and state primaries. It seems a pity that they will all probably go through life without being told that this is the week that the Swainson's thrush, on his way to the Canadian forests from Argentina, is passing through Guilford County.

May 14 – I have loaded the White Elephant

I have loaded the White Elephant and have once more joined the stream of pilgrims headed north, where the circumpolar arctic and subarctic forests and tundra, just awakening from a winter's sleep, wait to feed and support those who have the means to get there.

On my way west, I have stopped for a morning's fishing in the place that was the center of my life through the sometime carefree years, the Smith River of Virginia. I fish away the afternoon, through the old runs and riffles that hold more memories than trout on this day. As I watch the fly line follow the flow of this pool that Steve always insisted I fish first, it seems to me that contentment is where you find it, not necessarily waiting on the far side of the horizon. While I sought ever more exotic rivers and more and larger trout, I am certain that none of the days spent on the rivers of Montana and Alaska ever gave me more pleasure than those first ones, the best ones, when Steve and I lunched on vienna sausages and dreamed the dreams that were more sensibly left as fantasies by Steve but were pursued by me. At last I understand that it was the fellowship of the fishing as much as the fishing itself that made those days, just as it is the act of sharing anything that transforms. My companionship today is provided by Barney at my side, fishing with the same measured enthusiasm and blind faith as always, in these headwaters that led me to him in Montana.

> "...the end of all exploring
> Will be to arrive where we started
> And know the place for the first time."
> *Little Gidding,* T.S. Eliot

May 16—In acquiescence to the unhappy equation...

In acquiescence to the unhappy equation which states that in order to have wild, unspoiled country, I must leave my home, I have driven steadily since leaving. Late in this day I pause at the fringe of both East and West. Between Kansas City and Omaha I walk through a grove of shag-bark hickories and walnuts where the multi-colored warblers, back from the wintering grounds in Mexico, Central America, and the West Indies, flit through the feathery new foliage. I see cardinals, catbirds, a western tanager, and the eye-arresting red-headed woodpecker. As he slips through this pocket of hardwoods, the white secondaries on the back of each wing give his flight the same surrealistic, moth like quality as the fall ptarmigan of Alaska. This colorful woodpecker has been robbed of much of his habitat, the hardwood forest that once stretched from the eastern edge of the Great Plains to the sea. This grove brings to mind the descriptions of the eastern forests before the coming of the railroads.

"The eyes of the 'furrin' timber hunters must have popped with amazement as they rode the treacherous trails and creek banks of the plateau. On hundreds of such tucked-away places as Frozen Creek, the Bear Pen and Ball's Fork, he found a sparse population strung out along the banks of streams which still ran clear as crystal ..... The great poplars and whiteoaks grew, for the most part, near the base of the hills and in the coves, while the lesser oaks and chestnuts predominated on the sharper points and near the hilltops. Countless walnuts dotted the forest, thousands of them without blemish and a yard or more in diameter. The Goliaths were the superb, pencil-straight poplars, some of them towering one hundred and seventy-five feet and achieving a diameter of seven or eight feet. Next to these in value, if not in size, were the whiteoaks, which sometimes reached a thickness in excess of five feet. There were also the sturdy red, black and chestnut oaks and whole armies of tremendous hickories, huge but lovely beeches, "sugar trees" and maples, basswoods, an occasional ash, persimmon or black-gum, and lining the creek banks, the poetically graceful sycamores, birches and willows. And everywhere among the others were the mysterious, moody evergreens — the huge cedars, pines and hemlocks .... No region in earth's temperate zone boasts a larger variety of forest trees than the Cumberland Plateau, and in these years they abounded in natural profusion, little damaged by the avarice or caprice of men. The tree blights of the Old World had not yet infested this forest, and many specimens were centuries old and had withstood the fleeting decades without impairment. Tens of thousands of acres of such timber fell to the exploiters, from a people who, though they might fight each other with medieval brutality, at a business negotiation were as guileless as infants."[1]

[1] Harry M. Caudill, *Night Comes to the Cumberlands, A Biography of a Depressed Area,* Boston: Little, Brown and Company, 1963, foreword by Stewart L. Udall.

On this day, drove through Nebraska's Sand Hills which are the most extensive sand dune formation in the western hemisphere, and one of the only such formations that receives sufficient rainfall to be productive. In places the Sand Hills remind me of the foothills of the Rockies with their rolling grass parkland and scattered ponderosa pine. While some of the big dunes are a mile across, ten miles long and rise nearly 400 feet, the little 30 footers, called "choppies," seem to form an ocean of knobs, saddles, and humocks, mantled in the awakening pelage of spring.

America's tall grass prairie, once "The King of Prairies," covering 400,000 square miles, extended from Ohio to eastern Kansas and the Dakotas, from Texas into Canada. It has been turned into the corn belt, and exists only in a few isolated and shrinking pockets, and where Prairie Restorationists guard restored sites that they call "Noah's Arcs." While the tall grass prairie has gone the way of the bison, the greater prairie chicken and a host of other plant and animal species it supported, the short grass prairie that Barney and I drive through on this day feels like an inland sea. In the northwest corner of Nebraska, near Buffalo Gap National Grasslands, shimmering heat waves rise from Earth's broad, slumbering back like an aura. The bird song could be mistaken for the tinkling of thousands of wind chimes hidden in the grasses. The male lark bunting rises from his perch on a strand of barbed wire, then free falls, with his wings forming a graceful dihedral, back to the same perch. The silken whistle of the cowbird, the spiraling trill of the horned lark, passed through a diaphanous resonator of pure light, makes me feel as if bathed in a field of liberating energy. The ponds that lie in the swales of the grasslands are oases that ring with the piping of red-winged blackbirds and spring peepers. I see my first yellow-headed blackbird of the trip and know that Montana cannot be far.

I pick up a horned lark lying dead by the highway, marvelling at the little black "ears," the black, killdeer-like collar on the neck, the nails on each foot neat and sharp as needles. It was in Nebraska's Sand Hills region that Willa Cather, the writer, grew up and she never forgot the spell of the open prairie. (See journal entry for November 23.)

Along the highway I turn over fallen fence posts, looking for garter snakes, and from underneath each one, a meadow vole flashes down the "vole highways" that zigzag through the grass. Barney watches intently as I turn each post, then demonstrates his skill as a pouncing mouser. What was a vole becomes a furry vitamin pill, downed in an instant. I tell him that this mousing game should be beneath the dignity of a retriever of the regal pheasant and the lordly sage grouse, but his rapidly ticking tail tells me he will make up his own mind on such matters.

May 21—On this day Barney and I are back in Southwest Montana,

On this day Barney and I are back in southwest Montana, on Centenniel Creek, which runs high and dirty with snow melt, but is still fishable on this spring day. The willows are as bare as they were last fall when I fished this same water which ran low and clear in October. Overhead is a roaring of wind, but not, as last fall, as a precursor of the still, lifeless, gray days when the sun merely skirts the southern horizon, but as the harbinger of bursting life, stirring faintly in myriad seed pods, cocoons and mayfly larvae in the ground, on the bare willow branches, and under the stones of the riverbed. Yesterday I collected worms, the digging of which I think of as part of the complete brook trout fishing experience.

I have often asked myself where Barney draws the line as far as species which he considers worthy of his attention. He displays the same enthusiasm in catching an elegant grayling or urbane brown trout taken on a dry fly as in the collaring of a whitefish taken on a grub. Likewise, the malodorous common snipe is given the same respect as the aristocrat of game birds, the ruffed grouse. All creatures are accorded the same professional retrieve. However, when

Barney sees me breaking dirt clods apart in my hands and dropping the squirming morsels into his food dish, where the worms will be kept, he does not conceal his contempt for this strange ritual. Since I am sure he does not connect the act of worm digging with fishing later in the day, he must consider it quite pointless and bizarre.

I myself enjoy the act of worming immensely, and am always surprised by their quiet, but riotious lifestyle. The worms are prodigious lovers; fully one fourth of the ones I find are joined together in what the French call "Le Sport," and I rudely interrupt their lusty diversion.

Isaac Walton once stated that days spent fishing are not subtracted from one's lifetime. There is something akin to that same feeling of surreptitiously annexed wealth upon successfully abridging this purgatory of fishless days.

On this day I have come to the ranch where I worked as an irrigator in the spring and summer almost a decade ago. I give yesterday's catch of Centenniel Creek brook trout to the family that seated me at their table like one of their own. Barney and I then walk the fields and pastures where we two, equally new to Montana's fair country, had our first shared experiences. Sprinkler pipes now do my old job, and I look back on those pastoral days as ones I should have paid Lester for, rather than the reverse.

The irrigator is a man whose life is more visibly regulated by the sun than most. He rises with it, moving his canvas dams a hundred yards up the ditch to flood another section of field, makes another set when the sun is overhead, one more late in the afternoon, and one last move as the sun sinks out of sight. In the early morning the fields belong to him alone. No truck passes down the lane, raising dust. Man and his machines are quiet as the new day is formed. I remember walking through the flooded alfalfa, where the large wobbling droplets of water had cast out before my feet like silver chains, as I splashed across the fields to move the dams in the morning stillness. The magpies showed me how far the water had crept during the night. They hunt for earthworms which have been flushed from their cool passageways. They have no fear of me, knowing I carry only a shovel. The irrigator regulates the flow by making openings through the sides of the main ditch with the shovel. The water slices through these openings, hungry for new dryness. It moves down and across the field, pooling in the depressions. During the night it seeks out each foot of parched soil and in the morning, a whole section of the field shimmers with silver.

The birds are the voices and personalities of the different times of the irrigator's day. During the first changing of the dams, there is the uncertainty. I see the great horned owl, dark and sinister, planing soundlessly over the fields. It is his time of the day. As I make new openings in the main ditch, I watch the faint firing of the sky over the Ruby Range. Once the day is hot and the early colors have faded, I see a pewee on the barbed wire fence. He launches an attack on an insect, wingtips tapping loudly as he wheels and darts in pursuit. The kingfisher clatters noisily above the slough, flashing blue and white against the willows. The red shafted flicker drums on the snag of a cottonwood tree. I see his large brown eye studying me carefully. He flies, bouncing up and down in woodpecker-in-flight fashion. I hear his call come from far across the river, from a more lonely perch.

Walking the fields bearing only an innocent shovel, the irrigator is allowed to see the unfolding intimacies of the day in the flooded meadows. One rainy, blustery morning a fox trots across the field, his red fur dark with wetness. He is carrying a muskrat in his mouth. He sees me and begins to run, holding his tail full and high to catch the wind, fairly sailing out of sight with his prize. Often in the afternoon, a rainstorm will blow across the field toward Barney and me. When it is upon the two of us, to me it is only a coolness on the face and a relief from the mosquitos. Barney narrows his eyes in rapture as a river of scents flows by.

During the last changing of the dams, the night is gathering its strength and most of the birds are still. A strange disparity, the lonely cry of the killdeer and the clucking "laugh" of the common snipe are the last sounds I hear. I see the lights of ranch houses appear as pinpoints of light across the valley of the Beaverhead River. I suppose the same sounds are present in each of these nests of life. The mountains are still and silver, like a scene in an engraving. I hear the bark of a fox from far across the fields. I stand with the shovel over my shoulder, listening to the water whispering out of the ditch.

May 24 – On this day walked in the Crazy Mountains...

On this day walked in the Crazy Mountains north of the Yellowstone River, supposedly named by the mountain men after a woman who had made these mountains echo with her wailing after her family was killed by Indians in this small pocket of the Rockies. The dark tracts of timber are broken by balds and parklands. I sit, with Barney at my side, at the edges of these openings, in the new grass, and search for deer with my binoculars. The large herds periodically feed out into the open and then melt into the timber. The bucks have shed their horns and they move with uncharacteristic mildness among the does. I try to visit several mule deer winter range areas where the deer are concentrated each spring, to see the fawns, but mostly I use the occasion of fawn counting as an excuse to visit these places of "strong medicine" where the wind booms and the timber changes color from dark green to black as wayfaring clouds pass between the sun and me.

May 28 – Today I have returned to Yellowstone Park.

Today I have returned to Yellowstone Park, which seems to be emerging from a deep and fitful sleep. Though the road is clear, snow still lies in deep banks in the timber, and light snow showers briefly plunge the park back into its somnambulant state, on this day in May. I walk along the river, where the bison and elk, which were so fat and full of vitality last fall, walk dreamily through May's all enveloping trance. The torn hides and bones of animals that starved since I was here seven months ago lie as silent proof of the park's policy of non-intervention in nature's grim economics.

The Firehole River runs high and clear on this day, but other rivers in the park are already full and dirty with the spring freshet. I fish down through the same runs that Dad and I fished last fall, catching and releasing several brown trout that take the wet fly gently as it sweeps past the undercut bank. I see other fishermen, all early emergers who have waited for this moment for months, as they labored over their tying vises, preparing flies, and they spend their passion on these cold waters whose trout must wonder from what source does this sudden appearance of beautifully crafted arrangements of feather and fur, emanate. On this day, it is not the catching of fish that matters, but rather to be assured that this one pleasure remains as renewing as it has been in years past. On ponds and streams without number, fishermen are like pilgrims returning to their shrines, to cast their lines and rise from winter's ashes. While Yellowstone Park is not a place that is easily pushed out of one's mind by thoughts of a grander place, I find that my thoughts are drifting northward where I must prepare the boat, hang a new net, repair my engines, and put up my camp before I can relax. By now my friends in the village will be wondering if Barney and I will weather another summer on the hillside. We must not let them down.

June 8 — I have driven from Montana, across eastern Washington,

I have driven from Montana, across eastern Washington, where
the wind had created dust filled funnels that tower thousands of
feet into the sky. Like miniature tornados, the dust devils snake
their way across the sage brush flats and wheat fields. One such
twister had enveloped the White Elephant and I held the steering
wheel tightly as the bus shuttered and lurched. For an instant the
image of Dorothy and Toto being plucked from Kansas and deposited into the Land of Oz had flashed into my mind and I
laughed out loud, which earned a stern look from a nervous
Barney, who obviously felt that it was not the time for merriment.
Arrived in Seattle to learn that Melancholy Bay has had a late
break up of ice and the salmon periods are not expected to begin
until the third week in June. After taking a day to explore the sur-
prisingly wild beaches of Olympic National Park, west of Seattle,
drove the bus on the ferry at Anacortes, headed for Vancouver
Island, where Barney and I will spend one more week before head-
ing for another Melancholy summer.

As we drive up the island we explore logging roads that follow the rise of these mountains whose shoulders are washed by the Pacific. Across the valleys in the distance, the brooks that tumble down the mountainsides are long, white streamers cutting through the timber. In the high meadows, which are a perfect fantasy of wild flowers, Barney and I discover the arbutus trees, whose smooth, horn-like trunks are red against the conifers from a distance. On this day the hummingbirds dart among the arbutus' filigree of branches and I sit underneath and listen to their high, thin shrilling calls as they feed. If the gulls and soaring hawks could be called the children of the wind, giving it living form, then these rufous hummingbirds give form to the sun's rays. They seem to defy gravity as they levitate at the side of a blossom and then ricochet away like reflected light, the sound of their reedy, screeching calls following like trailing vapors. From the throat of the male shines a red incandescence of reflected light, but when clouds obscure the sun, the hummers seem to take umbrage and vanish.

While the bald eagle that wheels high over the island, with both the Strait of Georgia and the Strait of Juan de Fuca in view, is the obvious avian monarch, the band-tailed pigeons seem to lay claim to royal blood as well. They enter the valleys riding the winds that smell of the ocean in a most cavalier fashion, in flight that is one moment workmanlike and determined, and then, as if remembering that this island is long but narrow, they suddenly check themselves and settle into the top of a Douglas fir, where they survey this thin finger of coniferous forest that is Vancouver Island. Moments later, as if the view has not pleased them, the flock erupts into flight with a clattering of olive gray wings, only to settle a mile away in a still more pristine tree top.

Barney and I walk through the rainforests where all sounds, from the grinding of mossy stones underfoot, to the sound of the human voice, are rendered seductive and appealing. The sunlight streams through the branches of the conifers in shafts and from high overhead come the tinkling calls of chicadee and kinglet, one species seldom without the other in a symbiotic relationship I can only guess at. The sharp-shinned hawk, like a gray feathered arrow, bores through the interlaced branches in an eye-blink of motion.

The wind of a sudden rain squall moves through the needles of the firs as though they were the vocal chords of an assembled, waiting choir. The sound brings to mind Melancholy Bay, where the wind will soon be singing in the same key when it threads the mesh of my salmon net. There is something exhilarating in knowing that Barney and I are the first to smell this storm that has only known the ocean before striking land on this island poised at the edge of the Pacific Rim.

June 10 – On this day Barney and I explore the low tide beach...

On this day Barney and I explore the low tide beach at the southern end of Vancouver Island, where it is demonstrated that life can only be a chain of life underneath every rock I turn and in each tidal pool that I step over. The racing tide, using sand as an abrasive, has scoured out pockets and cavities in the boulders and in the mantle of rock that makes up much of this beach. In each pool, sculpin, rock crab and kelp flea wait for the next tidal cycle.

The forest that spills out onto the rocky beach is lush in a way that makes Melancholy Bay seem as barren as the moon. When Barney and I enter it, we push our way through a tanglefoot of fern and creeper, into the hemlock and fir. Along the rocky course of a stream are elegant silver alders, so different from the stunted ones of the thicket that will surround me in my tent shortly.

Back on the beach I sit on the logs and timbers that are riddled with the holes and burrows of shipworm and gribble. Several gray whales are in this cove and I watch for their spouts and glistening backs and flukes through my binoculars. Around thirty million years ago, some mammals, finding land not suited to their survival, returned to the sea, where they remained air breathing and warm blooded, nursing their young on milk. Having a lifespan comparable to man's, requiring twelve months for gestation and having the means to communicate vocally, the whale seems to be vitally linked to those who watch for them in these dark, fertile waters.

Nearly a decade ago in Baja California's Laguna San Ignacio, gray whale calves began to swim to the boats that sought them, to discover gentle, reaching hands. Other young whales began to follow their example and now a new relationship seems to be developing there. Perhaps it is similar to the 100th Monkey Syndrome, where, on one of the islands near Japan, once a body of approximately one hundred monkeys had learned to wash in the surf, the sand from the sweet potatoes left on the beaches for them by scientists studying their behavior, almost instantaneously, on all the other islands of the area, monkeys began washing their food in a like manner. At present, only Laguna San Ignacio whales are "friendly," but perhaps soon the required number will learn that Man, along this coastline where Mexico, the U.S., and Canada work together to preserve them, is no longer the enemy. Can we, come to intelligence much more recently than the leviathan, follow their example and learn that old enemies can become new friends? Sitting here in this perfect place, such thoughts come easily.

O God, my Master, should I gain the grace
To see Thee face to face when life is ended,
Grant that a little dog, who once pretended
That I was God, may see me face to face.
B.C.B.

East Woods Press Books

American Bed & Breakfast Cookbook, The
America's Grand Resort Hotels
Backcountry Cooking
Berkshire Trails for Walking & Ski Touring
Best Bed & Breakfast in the World, The
Blue Ridge Mountain Pleasures
California Bed & Breakfast Book, The
Campfire Chillers
Campfire Songs
Canoeing the Jersey Pine Barrens
Caribbean Bed & Breakfast Book, The
Carolina Curiosities
Carolina Seashells
Carpentry: Some Tricks of the Trade from an
    Old-Style Carpenter
Catch-of-the-Day — Southern Seafood Secrets
Catfish Cookbook, The
Charlotte: A Touch of Gold
Coastal Ghosts
Complete Guide to Backpacking in Canada
Creative Gift Wrapping
Day Trips From Baltimore
Day Trips From Cincinnati
Day Trips From Houston
Day Trips From Phoenix/Tucson
Drafting: Tips and Tricks on Drawing and
    Designing House Plans
Exploring Nova Scotia
Fifty Years on the Fifty: The Orange Bowl
    Story
Fructose Cookbook, The
Grand Old Ladies
Grand Strand: An Uncommon Guide to
    Myrtle Beach, The
Healthy Trail Food Book, The
Hiking from Inn to Inn: Maine to Virginia
Hiking Virginia's National Forests
Historic Country House Hotels in the U.K.
Hosteling USA, Third Edition
How to Afford Your Own Log Home
How to Play With Your Baby

Indiana: Off the Beaten Path
Interior Finish: More Tricks of the Trade
Just Folks: Visitin' with Carolina People
Kays Gary, Columnist
Maine Coast: A Nature Lover's Guide, The
Making Food Beautiful
Melancholy Bay, An Odyssey
Mid-Atlantic Guest House Book, The
New England Guest House Book, The
New England: Off the Beaten Path
Ohio: Off the Beaten Path
Parent Power!
Parks of the Pacific Coast
Race, Rock and Religion
River Reflections
Rocky Mountain National Park Hiking Trails
Saturday Notebook, The
Sea Islands of the South
Separation and Divorce in North Carolina
South Carolina Hiking Trails
Southern Guest House Book, The
Southern Rock: A Climber's Guide to the South
Sweets Without Guilt
Tar Heel Sights: Guide to North Carolina's Heritage
Tennessee Trails
Toys That Teach Your Child
Train Trips: Exploring America by Rail
Trout Fishing the Southern Appalachians
Vacationer's Guide to Orlando and Central Florida, A
Walks in the Catskills
Walks in the Great Smokies
Walks with Nature in Rocky Mountain National Park
Whitewater Rafting in Eastern America
Wildflower Folklore
Woman's Journey, A
You Can't Live on Radishes

Order from . . .

The East Woods Press

429 East Boulevard • Charlotte, NC 28203 • (704) 334-0897

For orders only, established accounts and charge card customers may call our toll-free answering service:
(800) 438-1242, ext. 102   In N.C. (800) 532-0476